1
9
9
2
-
9
3

STAR GUIDE™

1992-93

STAR GUIDE™

Published by:

Axiom
Information Resources
Ann Arbor, Michigan 48107

1992-1993 STAR GUIDE™
Published by Axiom Information Resources
Ann Arbor, Michigan 48107 USA

Copyright ©1991 Axiom Information Resources

Published by:
Axiom Information Resources
P.O. Box 8015
Ann Arbor, MI 48107

Printed in USA
ISBN # 0-943213-04-5

Cover Design by Kaleidoscope Art Works

SPECIAL SALES
The 1992-1993 STAR GUIDE™ is
available at special quantity discounts
for bulk purchases. For information write:

Axiom Information Resources
Marketing Dept. 7Q
P.O. Box 8015
Ann Arbor, MI 48107

Contents

Order Blanks and Customer Response Form (See Back Page)

INTRODUCTION

The aim of Star Guide™ 1992-1993 is to provide a complete list that acknowledges today's stars in all fields of human accomplishment along with their most accurate, up-to-date address. The universe of stars--a universe as diverse as General Norman Schwarzkopf, Spike Lee, Oprah Winfrey, George Will, Julia Roberts, Roseanne Barr-Arnold--is completely indexed, and alphabetically arranged under five convenient categories: Movie and TV, Music, Sports, Politics, and Other Famous People.

Star Guide™ 1992-1993 is a valuable communications tool that allows you and the stars to enjoy the human contact which is not possible through a star's performance or activity. With the Star Guide™, your favorite star can receive your praise, reassurance, criticism or offer of help. In return, stars often provide thanks, encouragement, recommendations, photos, autographs or other tokens of appreciation.

More than just a tool for the ordinary fan, the Star Guide™ is an invaluable resource tool for the reference librarian, collector, fund-raiser, trivia buff or anyone with any reason to contact a person of prominence.

Every reasonable effort has been made to ensure accurate addresses at press time, but stars obviously may move or change the circumstance by which they receive mail. Therefore, we cannot accept responsibility for inaccurate addresses. If there's a star you think should be listed but isn't write to us, and we'll try to include them in the next edition. Please remember, when writing to Axiom Information Resources, as well as when writing your favorite star, it is always best to enclose a self-addressed, stamped envelope. Please send your comments to Axiom Information Resources, P.O. Box 8015, Ann Arbor, MI 48107.

Star Guide's 1992-1993 Stars of the Year:

Movie.......... Kevin Costner
Television.... Bill Cosby
Music.......... Madonna
Sports.......... Michael Jordan
Politics....... President George Bush
Others......... General Norman Schwarzkope

Movies/TV

A _____ A

Beverly Aadland
P.O. Box 1115
Canyon Country, CA 91350

Willie Aames
12821 Moorpark #2
Studio City, CA 91604

Dihanne Abbott
460 West Avenue #46
Los Angeles, CA 90065

John Abbott
6424 Ivarene Avenue
Los Angeles, CA 90068

F. Murray Abraham
888 - 7th Ave. #1800
New York, NY 10019

Ray Abruzzo
20334 Pacific Coast Hwy.
Malibu, CA 90265

Sharon Acker
9744 Wilshire Blvd. #312
Beverly Hills, CA 90212

Bettye Ackerman
302 N. Alpine Drive
Beverly Hills, CA 90210

Leslie Ackerman
950 - 2nd Street #201
Santa Monica, CA 90403

Jay Acovone
151 S. El Camino Drive
Beverly Hills, CA 90212

Deborah Adair
10100 Santa Monica Blvd. #700
Los Angeles, CA 90067

Brooke Adams
2451 Holly Drive
Los Angeles, CA 90068

Joey Adams
1050 Fifth Avenue
New York, NY 10028

Julie Adams
5915 Corbin Avenue
Tarzana, CA 91356

Mason Adams
900 - 5th Avenue
New York, NY 10021

Maud Adams
12700 Ventura Blvd. #350
Studio City, CA 91604

Isabelle Adjani
2 rue Gaston de St. Paul
75016, Paris, FRANCE

Iris Adrian
3341 Floyd Terrace
Los Angeles, CA 90028

John Agar
639 N. Hollywood Way
Burbank, CA 91505

Jenny Agutter
6882 Camrose Drive
Los Angeles, CA 90068

Charles Aidman
525 N. Palm Drive
Beverly Hills, CA 90210

Danny Aiello
4 Thornhill Drive
Ramsey, NJ 07446

Claude Akins
1927 Midlothian Drive
Altadena, CA 91001

Eddie Albert
719 Amalfi Drive
Pacific Palisades, CA 90272

Edward Albert
10100 Santa Monica #1600
Los Angeles, CA 90067

Dolores Albin
13006 Woodbridge
Studio City, CA 91604

Alan Alda
100 Universal Plaza Blvd. #507
Universal City, CA 91608

Frank Aletter
5430 Corbin Avenue
Tarzana, CA 91356

Denise Alexander
345 N. Maple Drive #183
Beverly Hills, CA 90210

Jane Alexander
Gordon Road, RFD #2
Carmel, NY 10512

Kristian Alfonso
P.O. Box 93-1628
Los Angeles, CA 90093

Ana-Alicia
9744 Wilshire Blvd. #308
Beverly Hills, CA 90212

Jed Allan
11759 Iowa Avenue
Los Angeles, CA 90025

Byron Allen
1875 Century Park E. #2200
Los Angeles, CA 90067

Chad Allen
12049 Smokey Lane
Cerritos, CA 90701

Corey Allen
8642 Hollywood Blvd.
Los Angeles, CA 90046

Debbie Allen
607 Marguerita Avenue
Santa Monica, CA 90402

Karen Allen
122 E. 10th Street
New York, NY 10013

Nancy Allen
409 N. Camden Drive #105
Beverly Hills, CA 90210

John Amos
431 W. 162nd Street
New York, NY 10032

Sean Barbara Allen
1622 Sierra Bonita Avenue
Los Angeles, CA 90046

Morey Amsterdam
1012 N. Hillcrest Road
Beverly Hills, CA 90210

Steve Allen
16185 Woodvale Road
Encino, CA 91316

Barbara Anderson
4345 Enoro Drive
Los Angeles, CA 90008

Woody Allen
930 Fifth Avenue
New York, NY 10018

Dame Judith Anderson
808 San Ysidro Lane
Santa Barbara, CA 93013

Kirstie Alley
4875 Louise
Encino, CA 91316

Loni Anderson
1001 Indiantown Road
Jupiter, FL 33458

Christopher Allport
121 N. San Vincente Blvd.
Beverly Hills, CA 90211

Melissa Sue Anderson
20722 Pacific Coast Hwy.
Malibu, CA 90265

June Allyson
1651 Foothill Road
Ojai, CA 93020

Melody Anderson
10433 Wilshire Blvd. #1203
Los Angeles, CA 90024

Maria Conchita Alonso
9455 Eden Place
Beverly Hills, CA 90210

Michael Anderson, Jr.
132B S. Lasky Drive
Beverly Hills, CA 90212

Don Ameche
2121 Avenue of the Americas #950
Los Angeles, CA 90067

Richard Anderson
10120 Cielo Drive
Beverly Hills, CA 90210

Leon Ames
1015 Goldenrod Avenue
Corona del Mar, CA 92625

Richard Dean Anderson
2400 Boundry Road
Burnaby, BC V5M 2Z3, CANADA

Ursula Andress
Danikhofenweg 95
3072 Ostermundingen,
SWITZERLAND

Dana Andrews
4238 Beeman Avenue
Studio City, CA 91603

Tige Andrews
4914 Encino Terrace
Encino, CA 91316

Annabella
1 rue Pierret
92200 Neuilly FRANCE

Michael Ansara
4624 Park Mirasol
Calabasas, CA 91302

Susan Anspach
473 - 16th Street
Santa Monica, CA 90402

Susan Anton
1853 Noel Place
Beverly Hills, CA 90210

Christina Applegate
4527 Park Allegra
Calabasas, CA 91302

Anne Archer
13201 Old Oak Lane
Los Angeles, CA 90049

Adam Arkin
50 Ridge Drive
Chappaqua, NY 10514

Bess Armstrong
1518 N. Doheny Drive.
Los Angeles, CA 90069

Curtis Armstrong
6306 Ivarene
Los Angeles, CA 90068

Desi Arnaz, Jr.
P.O. Box 2000
Ojai, CA 93023

Lucie Arnaz
560 Tigertail Road
Los Angeles, CA 90049

James Arness
P.O. Box 49003
Los Angeles, CA 90049

Rosanna Arquette
13596 Contour Drive
Sherman Oak, CA 91423

Beatrice Arthur
2000 Old Ranch Road
Los Angeles, CA 90049

Dana Ashbrook
335 N. Maple Drive #250
Beverly Hills, CA 90210

Elizabeth Ashley
9010 Dorrington Avenue
Los Angeles, CA 90048

Jennifer Ashley
200 N Robertson Blvd. #219
Beverly Hills, CA 90211

Edward Asner
P.O. Box 7407
Studio City, CA 91614

Rene Auberjonois
448 S. Arden Blvd.
Los Angeles, CA 90020

Armand Assante
Route 1, Box 561
Campbell Hall, NY 10916

Karen Austin
141 El Camino Drive #205
Beverly Hills, CA 90212

John Astin
1271 Stoner Avenue #4408
Los Angeles, CA 90024

Dan Aykroyd
3960 Laurel Canyon Blvd.
Studio City, CA 91604

Sean Astin
17815 Valley Vista
Encino, CA 91436

Lew Ayres
675 Walther Way
Los Angeles, CA 90049

Christopher Atkins
3751 Sunswept Drive
Studio City, CA 91604

Candy Azzara
1155 N. La Cienega Blvd. #307
Los Angeles, CA 90069

B   B

Lauren Bacall
1 W. 72nd Street #43
New York, NY 10023

Max Baer, Jr.
10433 Wilshire Blvd. #103
Los Angeles, CA 90024

Catherine Bach
14000 Davana Terrace
Sherman Oaks, CA 91403

Barbara Bain
23717 Long Valley Road
Calabasas, CA 91302

Kevin Bacon
800 West End Avenue #7A
New York, NY 10025

Conrad Bain
1230 Chickory Lane
Los Angeles, CA 90049

Jane Badler
8383 Wilshire Blvd. #840
Beverly Hills, CA 90211

Scott Baio
3130 Dona Sarita Place
Studio City, CA 91604

Joe Don Baker
23339 Hatteras
Woodland Hills, CA 91364

Alec Baldwin
300 Central Park West
New York, NY 10024

Kaye Ballard
211 E. 70th Street #20C
New York, NY 10021

Martin Balsam
c/o Hotel Olcott
27 W. 72nd Street
New York, NY 10011

Anne Bancroft
2301 La Mesa Drive
Santa Monica, CA 90405

Brigitte Bardot
83990 La Madrigue
St. Tropez, VAR FRANCE

Bob Barker
1851 Outpost Drive
Los Angeles, CA 90068

Ellen Barkin
8185 Gould Avenue
Los Angeles, CA 90046

Priscilla Barnes
3500 Olive Avenue #1400
Burbank, CA 91505

Doug Barr
515 S. Irving Blvd.
Los Angeles, CA 90020

Roseanne Barr-Arnold
12916 Evanston
Los Angeles, CA 90049

Barbara Barrie
465 West End Avenue
New York, NY 10024

Chuck Barris
1990 Bundy Avenue
Los Angeles, CA 90025

Drew Barrymore
3960 Laurel Canyon #159
Studio City, CA 91604

Billy Barty
4502 Farmdale Avenue
North Hollywood, CA 91602

Kim Basinger
345 N. Maple Drive #373
Beverly Hills, CA 90210

Jason Bateman
2628 - 2nd Street
Santa Monica, CA 90405

Justine Bateman
3960 Laurel Canyon #193
Studio City, CA 91604

Steven Bauer
5233 Strohm Avenue
North Hollywood, CA 91601

Jennifer Beals
8899 Beverly Blvd.
Los Angeles, CA 90048

Allyce Beasley
2415 Castilion Drive
Los Angeles, CA 90068

Ned Beatty
2706 N. Beachwood Drive
Los Angeles, CA 90027

Warren Beatty
13671 Mulholland Drive
Beverly Hills, CA 90210

Bonnie Bedella
1021 Georgina Avenue
Santa Monica, CA 90402

Leslie Bega
6451 Deep Dell Place
Los Angeles, CA 90048

Shari Belafonte-Harper
3546 Longridge Avenue
Sherman Oaks, CA 91423

Barbara Bel Geddes
11 Mill Street
Putnam Vally, NY 10579

Kathleen Beller
2018 N. Whitley Avenue
Los Angeles, CA 90068

Jean-Paul Belmondo
77 Ave. Donfert Rochereaux
Paris, 16, FRANCE

James Belushi
9830 Wilshire Blvd
Beverly Hills, CA 90212

Dirk Benedict
1637 Willesley Drive
Santa Monica, CA 90406

Richard Benjamin
719 N. Foothill Road
Beverly Hills, CA 90210

Barbi Benton
P.O. Box 549
Carbondale, CO 81623

Tom Berenger
P.O. Box 1842
Beaufort, SC 29901

Candice Bergen
8436 W. 3rd Street #650
Los Angeles, CA 90048

Sandahl Bergman
9903 Santa Monica Blvd. #274
Beverly Hills, CA 90212

Milton Berle
10750 Wilshire Blvd. #1003
Los Angeles, CA 90024

Crystal Bernard
10100 Santa Monica Blvd. #1600
Los Angeles, CA 90067

Corbin Bernsen
3500 W. Olive #920
Burbank, CA 91505

Ken Berry
1900 Outpost Drive
Los Angeles, CA 90068

Star Guide 1992-1993   TV/Movies

Valerie Bertinelli
15760 Ventura Blvd. #700
Encino, CA 91436

Robert Blake
11604 Dilling Street
North Hollywood, CA 91608

James Best
9744 Wilshire Blvd. #306
Beverly Hills, CA 90212

Susan Blakely
8383 Wilshire Blvd. #840
Beverly Hills, CA 90211

Michael Biehn
3737 Deervale Drive
Sherman Oaks, CA 91403

Tempest Bledsoe
8230 Beverly Blvd. #23
Los Angeles, CA 90048

Barbara Billingsley
8000 San Lorenzo Street
San Monica, CA 90402

Claire Bloom
109 Jermyn Street
London, W1, ENGLAND

David Birney
20 Ocean Park Blvd. #11
Santa Monica, CA 90405

Lindsay Bloom
3751 Reklaw
Studio City, CA 91604

Joey Bishop
534 Via Lido Nord
Newport Beach, CA 92660

Heidi Bohay
4304 Farmdale Avenue
Studio City, CA 91604

Jacqueline Bisset
1815 Benedict Canyon Drive
Beverly Hills, CA 90210

Joe Bologna
613 N. Arden Drive
Beverly Hills, CA 90210

Bill Bixby
200 N. Robertson Blvd. #223
Beverly Hills, CA 90211

Lisa Bonet
6435 Balcom
Reseda, CA 91335

Honor Blackman
8 Harley Street
London, W1N 2AB, ENGLAND

Ernest Borgnine
3055 Lake Glen Drive
Beverly Hills, CA 90210

Linda Blair
8033 Sunset Blvd. #204
Los Angeles, CA 90046

Tom Bosley
2822 Royston Place
Beverly Hills, CA 90210

11

Star Guide 1992-1993   TV/Movies

Barry Bostwick
2770 Hutton Drive
Beverly Hills, CA 90210

Judi Bowker
31 Soho Square
London, W1, ENGLAND

Bruce Boxleitner
24500 John Colter Road
Hidden Hills, CA 91302

Lorraine Bracco
P.O. Box 49
Palisades, NY 10964

Ed Bradley
555 W. 57th Street
New York, NY 10019

Marlon Brando
P.O. Box 809
Beverly Hills, CA 90213

Eileen Brennan
P.O. Box 1777
Ojai, CA 93023

David Brenner
229 E. 62nd Street
New York, NY 10021

Beau Bridges
5525 N. Jed Smith Road
Hidden Hills, CA 91302

Jeff Bridges
436 Adelaide
Santa Monica, CA 90402

Lloyd Bridges
225 Loring Avenue
Los Angeles, CA 90077

Todd Bridges
7550 Zombar Avenue #1
Van Nuys, CA 91406

David Brinkley
1717 DeSales Street
Washington, DC 20036

Danielle Brisebois
9255 Sunset Blvd. #603
Los Angeles, CA 90069

Morgan Brittany
c/o S. Sauer Enterprisers
2029 Century Park East
Los Angeles, CA 90067

Matthew Broderick
3908 Fairway
Studio City, CA 91604

Tom Brokaw
941 Park Ave. #14C
New York, NY 10025

James Brolin
803 Country Club Drive
Ojai, CA 93023

Charles Bronson
P.O. Box 2644
Malibu, CA 90265

Albert Brooks
3600 Longridge Avenue
Sherman Oaks, CA 91403

12

Mel Brooks
2301 La Mesa Drive
Santa Monica, CA 90405

Randi Brooks
2458 Creston Way
Los Angeles, CA 90068

Pierce Brosnan
28011 N. Parquet Place
Malibu, CA 90265

Blair Brown
8899 Beverly Blvd.
Los Angeles, CA 90048

Georg Stanford Brown
2934 1/2 Beverly Glen Court #404
Los Angeles, CA 90077

Genevieve Bujold
27258 Pacific Coast Hwy.
Malibu, CA 90265

Carol Burnett
P.O. Box 1298
South Pasadena, CA 91031

George Burns
720 N. Maple Drive
Beverly Hills, CA 90210

Raymond Burr
P.O. Box 678
Geyserville, CA 95441

Ellen Burstyn
Ferry House, Box 217
Washington Spring Road
Palisades, NY 10964

Gary Busey
2914 Searidge Street
Malibu, CA 90265

Timothy Busfield
2416 "G" Street #D
Sacramento, CA 95816

C   C

James Caan
1435 Stone Canyon Road
Los Angeles, CA 90077

Sid Caesar
1910 Loma Vista Drive
Beverly Hills, CA 90210

Nicholas Cage
5647 Tryon
Los Angeles, CA 90068

Michael Caine
Rectory Farm House
N. Stoke Oxfordshire ENGLAND

Kirk Cameron
1450 Belfast Drive
Los Angeles, CA 90069

Colleen Camp
2050 Fairburn Avenue
Los Angeles, CA 90025

John Candy
11454 San Vicente Blvd.
Los Angeles, CA 90049

Dyan Cannon
8033 Sunset Blvd. #254
Los Angeles, CA 90046

Diana Canova
8370 Wilshire Blvd. #310
Beverly Hills, CA 90211

Kate Capshaw
709 - 19th Street
Santa Monica, CA 90402

George Carlin
901 Bringham Avenue
Los Angeles, CA 90049

Art Carney
RR 20, Box 911
Westbrook, CT 06498

David Carradine
9753 La Tuna Canyon Road
Sun Valley, CA 91352

Keith Carradine
20800 Hillside Drive
Topanga, CA 90290

Robert Carradine
2121 Avenue of the Stars #950
Los Angeles, CA 90067

Barbara Carrera
15430 Milldale Drive
Los Angeles, CA 90077

Diahann Carroll
P.O. Box 2999
Beverly Hills, CA 90213

Johnny Carson
6962 Wildlife Road
Malibu, CA 90265

Dixie Carter
618 S. Lucerne Blvd.
Los Angeles, CA 90005

Lynda Carter
9200 Harrington Drive
Potomac, MD 20854

Nell Carter
13360 Java Drive
Beverly Hills, CA 90210

Angela Cartwright
10112 Riverside Drive
Toluca Lake, CA 91602

Bernie Casey
10100 Santa Monica Blvd. #1600
Los Angeles, CA 90067

Joanna Cassidy
463 Mesa Road
Santa Monica, CA 90402

Patrick Cassidy
10433 Wilshire Blvd. #605
Los Angeles, CA 90024

Phoebe Cates
136 E. 57th Street #1001
New York, NY 10022

Star Guide 1992-1993

Kim Cattrall
760 N. La Cienega Blvd.
Los Angeles, CA 90069

Max Caufield
4036 Foothill Road
Carpenteria, CA 93013

Dick Cavett
2200 Fletcher Avenue
Ft. Lee, NJ 07024

Christopher Cazenove
9169 Sunset Blvd.
Los Angeles, CA 90069

Richard Chamberlain
87/829 Farrington Hwy.
Waianae, HI 96792

Marilyn Chambers
4528 W. Charleston Blvd.
Las Vegas, NV 89102

Marge Champion
484 W. 43rd Street
New York, NY 10036

Carol Channing
9301 Flicker Way
Los Angeles, CA 90069

Stockard Channing
10390 Santa Monica Blvd. #300
Los Angeles, CA 90025

Rosalind Chao
201 Ocean Avenue #506-P
Santa Monica, CA 90402

Cyd Charisse
10390 Wilshire Blvd. #1507
Los Angeles, CA 90024

Charro (Rasten)
P.O. Box 1007
Hanalei Kaui, HI 96714

Chevy Chase
2916 Main Street #200
Santa Monica, CA 90405

Cher
9200 Sunset Blvd. #1001
Los Angeles, CA 90069

Rae Dawn Chong
P.O. Box 181
Bearsville, NY 12409

Julie Christie
23 Linden Gardens
London, W2, ENGLAND

William Christopher
P.O. Box 50698
Pasadena, CA 91105

Connie Chung
1 W. 72 Street
New York, NY 10023

Andrew Dice Clay
48 E. 50th Street #400
New York, NY 10022

Jill Clayburgh
225 McLain Street
Mt. Kisco, NY 10549

John Cleese
82 Ladbroke Road
London, W11 3NU, ENGLAND

Rosemary Clooney
1019 N. Roxbury Drive
Beverly Hills, CA 90210

Glenn Close
9830 Wilshire Blvd.
Beverly Hills, CA 90212

James Coburn
3930 Holly Lane Drive
Sherman Oaks, CA 91403

Imogene Coca
200 E. 66th Street #1803D
New York, NY 10021

Claudette Colbert
Bellerive St. Peter
Barbados, WEST INDIES

Michael Cole
6332 Costello Avenue
Van Nuys, CA 91401

Dabney Coleman
360 N. Kenter Avenue
Los Angeles, CA 90049

Gary Coleman
900 Sunset Blvd. #1200
Los Angeles, CA 90069

Gary Collins
2751 Hutton Place
Beverly Hills, CA 90212

Joan Collins
19 Eaton Place # 2
London, SW1, ENGLAND

Stephen Collins
7920 Sunset Blvd. #350
Los Angeles, CA 90046

Sean Connery
Casa Malibu, Fuente Del Rodeo
Nueva, Andalusia
Malaga, SPAIN

Carol Connors
1709 Ferrari Drive
Beverly Hills, CA 90210

Chuck Connors
HC 99 - Box 4400-73
Tehachapi, CA 93561

Mike Connors
4810 Louise Avenue
Encino, CA 91316

Robert Conrad
4625 Petit Avenue
Encino, CA 91316

William Conrad
4031 Longridge
Sherman Oaks, CA 91403

Michael Constantine
17 Blvd. Bartole, Beauvallen
83120 Saint Maxime, FRANCE

Tom Conti
Chatto
Shaftesbury Avenue
London, W1, ENGLAND

Gary Conway
2035 Mandeville Canyon
Los Angeles, CA 90049

Kevin Conway
9229 Sunset Blvd. #607
Los Angeles, CA 90069

Tim Conway
P.O. Box 17047
Encino, CA 91416

Elisha Cook, Jr.
429 Mandich Lane, Box 335
Bishop, CA 93514

Jackie Cooper
9621 Royalton
Beverly Hills, CA 90210

Teri Copley
4535 Coldwater #103
North Hollywood, CA 91604

Ellen Corby
9026 Harratt Street
Los Angeles, CA 90069

Alex Cord
10100 Santa Monica Blvd. #700
Los Angeles, CA 90067

Don Cornelius
214 St. Pierre Road
Los Angeles, CA 90024

Bud Cort
666 N. Larchmont Blvd. #309
Los Angeles, CA 90004

Bill Cosby
34-12 - 36th Street
Astoria, NY 11106

Kevin Costner
P.O. Box 772
La Canada, CA 91011

Joseph Cotton
1993 Mesa drive
Palm Springs, CA 92264

Katie Couric
30 Rockefeller Plaza #304
New York, NY 10020

Courtney Cox
9016 Wilshire Blvd. #500
Beverly Hills, CA 90211

Ronnie Cox
13948 Magnolia Blvd.
Sherman Oaks, CA 91423

Yvonne Craig
1221 Ocean Avenue #202
Santa Monica, CA 90401

Richard Crenna
3951 Valley Meadow Road
Encino, CA 91316

Walter Cronkite
519 E. 84th Street
New York, NY 10028

Hume Cronyn
63-23 Carlton Street
Rego Park, NY 11374

Cathy Lee Crosby
1223 Wilshire Blvd. #404
Santa Monica, CA 90403

Mary Crosby
2875 Barrymore
Malibu, CA 90265

Norm Crosby
1400 Londonderry Place
Los Angeles, CA 90069

Tom Cruise
14775 Ventura Blvd. #1-710
Sherman Oaks, CA 91403

Billy Crystal
860 Chautauqua Blvd.
Pacific Palisades, CA 90272

Robert Culp
357 Crown Drive
Los Angeles, CA 90049

Lee Curreri
24 1/2 Park Avenue
Venice, CA 90291

Tim Curry
2401 Wild Oak Drive
Los Angeles, CA 90068

Jane Curtin
35 West 11th Street
New York, NY 10011

Valerie Curtin
15622 Meadowgate Road
Encino, CA 91316

Jamie Lee Curtis
1242 S. Camden Drive
Los Angeles, CA 90035

Tony Curtis
P.O. Box 540
Beverly Hills, CA 90213

John Cusack
8451 Melrose Place #200
Los Angeles, CA 90069

Peter Cushing
Seasalter Whitstable
Kent, ENGLAND

D   D

Maryam D'Abo
9301 Wilshire Blvd. #312
Beverly Hills, CA 90210

Olivia d'Abo
7495 Mulholland Drive
Los Angeles, CA 90046

Willem Dafoe
33 Wooster Street #200
New York, NY 10013

Timothy Dalton
15 Golden Square #315
London, W1, ENGLAND

Tyne Daly
2934 1/2 Beverly Glen Ct. #404
Los Angeles, CA 90077

Beverly D'Angelo
2168 Outpost
Los Angeles, CA 90068

Rodney Dangerfield
1118 - 1st Avenue
New York, NY 10021

Blyth Danner
304 - 21st Street
Santa Monica, CA 90402

Ted Danson
9830 Wilshire Blvd.
Beverly Hills, CA 90212

Tony Danza
25000 Malibu Road
Malibu, CA 90265

Patti D'Arbanville
432 - 15th Street
Santa Monica, CA 90403

James Darren
P.O. Box 1088
Beverly Hills, CA 90213

John Davidson
6051 Spring Valley Road
Hidden Hills, CA 91302

Clifton Davis
24042 E. Falcon View
Diamond Bar, CA 91765

Geena Davis
8033 Sunset Blvd. #367.
Los Angeles, CA 90046

Mac Davis
759 Nimes Road
Los Angeles, CA 90077

Ossie Davis & Ruby Dee
44 Cortland Avenue
New Rochelle, NY 10801

Pam Dawber
2236-A Encinitas Blvd.
Encinitas, CA 92024

Doris Day
P.O. Box 223163
Carmel, CA 93922

Yvonne DeCarlo
300A High Point #601
Hartsdale, NY 10540

Sandra Dee
10780 Santa Monica Blvd. #280
Los Angeles, CA 90025

Olivia DeHavilland
Boite Postale 156-16
75764 Paris, Cedex 16, FRANCE

Dana Delany
3435 Ocean Park Blvd. #201-N
Santa Monica, CA 90405

Dom Deluise
1186 Corsica Drive
Pacific Palisades, CA 90272

Rebecca DeMornay
2179 Castilian Drive
Los Angeles, CA 90068

Patrick Dempsey
431 Lincoln Blvd.
Santa Monica, CA 90402

Catherine Deneuve
76 Rue Bonaparte
Paris, 6, FRANCE

Robert DeNiro
1501 Broadway #2600
New York, NY 10036

Brian Dennehy
121 N. San Vicente Blvd.
Beverly Hills, CA 90211

Bob Denver
901 Brush Street
Las Vegas, NV 89107

Bo Derek
3625 Roblar
Santa Ynez, CA 93460

Bruce Dern
23430 Malibu Colony Road
Malibu, CA 90265

Laura Dern
760 N. La Cienega Blvd.
Los Angeles, CA 90069

William Devane
15027 Valley Vista
Sherman Oaks, CA 91403

Danny DeVito
31020 Broad Beach Road
Malibu, CA 90265

Joyce DeWitt
101 Ocean Avenue #L-4
Santa Monica, CA 90402

Susan Dey
10390 Santa Monica Blvd. #300
Los Angeles, CA 90025

Angie Dickinson
9580 Lime Orchard Road
Beverly Hills, CA 90210

Marlene Dietrich
12 Avenue Montaigne
75008 (8 EME) Paris, FRANCE

Phyliss Diller
163 S. Rockingham Road
Los Angeles, CA 90049

Kevin Dillon
49 W. 9th Street
New York, NY 10010

Matt Dillon
49 W. 9th Street
New York, NY 10010

Donna Dixon
8955 Norma Place
Los Angeles, CA 90069

Kevin Dobson
11930 Iredell Street
Studio City, CA 91604

Elinor Donahue
4525 Lemp Avenue
North Hollywood, CA 91602

Phil Donahue
420 E. 54th Street #22F
New York, NY 10022

Troy Donahue
1022 Euclid Avenue #1
Santa Monica, CA 90403

Amanda Donohue
8899 Beverly Blvd.
Los Angelesw, CA 90048

James Doohan
5533 Matilija Avenue
Van Nuys, CA 91401

Kirk Douglas
805 N. Rexford Drive
Beverly Hills, CA 90210

Michael Douglas
P.O. Box 49054
Los Angeles, CA 90049

Mike Douglas
602 North Arden Drive
Beverly Hills, CA 90210

Robyn Douglas
1355 N. Sandburg Terrace
Chicago, IL 60610

Leslie-Ann Down
6509 Wandermere Road
Malibu, CA 90265

Robert Downey, Jr.
1494 N. Kings Road
Los Angeles, CA 90069

Hugh Downs
P.O. Box 1132
Carefree, AZ 85331

Richard Dreyfuss
2809 Nichols Canyon
Los Angeles, CA 90046

Fred Dryer
11911 Mayfield Avenue
Los Angeles, CA 90049

Ja' Net Dubois
6310 San Vicente Blvd. #407
Los Angeles, CA 90048

Julia Duffy
10100 Santa Monica Blvd. #700
Los Angeles, CA 90067

Patrick Duffy
P.O. Box "D"
Tarzana, CA 91356

Olympia Dukakis
222 Upper Mountain Road
Montclair, NJ 07043

Patty Duke
17815 Valley Vista Blvd.
Encino, CA 91316

David Dukes
255 S. Lorraine Blvd.
Los Angeles, CA 90004

Faye Dunaway
1435 Linda Crest Drive
Beverly Hills, CA 90210

Deanna Durbin
B.P. 767
75123 Paris Cedex 03, FRANCE

Charles Durning
10590 Wilshire Blvd. #506
Los Angeles, CA 90024

Marj Dusay
1930 Century Park East #303
Los Angeles, CA 90067

Robert Duvall
257 W. 86th Street #5B
New York, NY 10024

Shelly Duvall
12725 Ventura Blvd.
Studio City, CA 91604

E   E

Clint Eastwood
4000 Warner Blvd. #16
Burbank, CA 91522

Roger Ebert
2114 N. Cleveland
Chicago, IL 60614

Buddy Ebsen
605 via Horquilla
Palos Verdes Estates, CA 90274

Barbara Eden
9816 Denbigh
Beverly Hills, CA 90210

Anthony Edwards
8820 Lookout Mountain
Los Angeles, CA 90046

Samantha Eggar
15430 Mulholland Drive
Los Angeles, CA 90024

Beth Ehlers
233 E. 88th Street
New York, NY 10028

Jill Eikenberry
2183 Mandeville Canyon
Los Angeles, CA 90049

Jack Elam
P.O. Box 5718
Santa Barbara, CA 93108

Sam Elliott
33050 Pacific Coast Hwy.
Malibu, CA 90265

Emilio Estevez
31709 Sea Level Drive
Malibu, CA 90265

Erik Estrada
3768 Eureka Drive
Studio City, CA 91604

Bob Eubanks
23801 Calabasas Road #2050
Calabasas, CA 91302

Chad Everett
19901 Northridge Road
Chatsworth, CA 91311

Dale Evans (Rogers)
15650 Seneca Road
Victorville, CA 92392

Greg Evigan
5070 Arundel Drive
Woodland Hills, CA 91364

Linda Evans
6015 W. 6th Street
Los Angeles, CA 90036

Tom Ewell
57 Aspen Street
Rolling Hills Estates, CA 90274

F   F

Shelley Fabares
P.O. Box 6010 #85
Sherman Oaks, CA 91413

Debrah Farentino
586 Lorna Lane
Los Angeles, CA 90049

Clifton Fadiman
3222 Campanil Drive
Santa Barbara, CA 93109

Shannon Farnon
12743 Milbank Street
Studio City, CA 91604

Bruce Fairbairn
9744 Wilshire Blvd. #308
Beverly Hills, CA 90212

Richard Farnsworth
3219 Ellington Drive
Los Angeles, CA 90068

Douglas Fairbanks, Jr.
575 Park Avenue
New York, NY 10021

Felicia Farr
141 S. El Camino Drive #201
Beverly Hills, CA 90212

Morgan Fairchild
3321 Dixie Canyon Lane
Beverly Hills, CA 90210

Jamie Farr
53 Ranchero
Bell Canyon, CA 91307

Peter Falk
1004 N. Roxbury Drive
Beverly Hills, CA 90210

Mike Farrell
P.O. Box 5961-306
Sherman Oaks, CA 91413

Shea Farrell
125 Bowling Green Way
Los Angeles, CA 90049

Mia Farrow
135 Central Park West
New York, NY 10018

Farrah Fawcett
3130 Antelo Road
Los Angeles, CA 90077

Alice Faye
49400 JFK Trail
Palm Desert, CA 92260

Alan Feinstein
432 S. Ogden Drive
Los Angeles, CA 90036

Fritz Feld
12348 Rochedale
Los Angeles, CA 90049

Corey Feldman
454 N. Oakhurst Drive
Beverly Hills, CA 90210

Barbara Feldon
14 E. 74th Street
New York, NY 10021

Norman Fell
4314 Marina City Drive #1020
Marina del Rey, CA 90292

Edith Fellows
2016 1/2 N. Vista Del Mar
Los Angeles, CA 90068

Sherilyn Fenn
7266 Franklin Avenue #310
Los Angeles, CA 90046

George Fenneman
13214 Moorpark #206
Sherman Oaks, CA 91423

Conchata Ferrell
1347 N. Sewart Street
Los Angeles, CA 90028

Jose Ferrer
P.O Box 616
Miami, FL 33133

Mel Ferrer
6590 Camino Carreta
Carpinteria, CA 93013

Lou Ferrigno
621 - 17th Street
Santa Monica, CA 90402

Sally Field
825 S. Barrington Avenue #204
Los Angeles, CA 90049

Sylvia Field
3263 Via Alta Mira
Fallbrook, CA 92028

Virginia Field-Parker
74580 Fairway Drive
Indian Wells, CA 92260

Kim Fields
23460 Hatteras Street
Woodland Hills, CA 91367

Albert Finney
388 Oxford Street
London, W1, ENGLAND

Peter Firth
4 Windmill Street
London, W1, ENGLAND

Carrie Fisher
9555 Oak Pass Road
Beverly Hills, CA 90210

Gail Fisher
1150 S. Hayworth
Los Angeles, CA 90035

Fionnula Flanagan
13438 Java Drive
Beverly Hills, CA 90210

Susan Flannery
480 Pimiento Lane
Santa Barbara, CA 93108

Rhonda Fleming-Mann
2129 Century Woods Way
Los Angeles, CA 90067

Louise Fletcher
1520 Camden Avenue #105
Los Angeles, CA 90025

Nina Foch
P.O. Box 1884
Beverly Hills, CA 90213

Jane Fonda
914 Montana Avenue #200
Santa Monica, CA 90402

Peter Fonda
RR #38
Livingston, MT 59047

Joan Fontaine
P.O. Box 222600
Carmel, CA 93922

Faith Ford
151 El Camino
Beverly Hills, CA 90212

Glenn Ford
911 Oxford Way
Beverly Hills, CA 90210

Harrison Ford
P.O. Box 49344
Los Angeles, CA 90049

Stephen Ford
Rt #1, Box 90
San Luis Obispo, CA 93401

Robert Forster
8550 Holloway Drive #402
Los Angeles, CA 90069

John Forsythe
14215 Sunset Blvd.
Pacific Palisades, CA 90272

Fabian Forte
6671 Sunset Blvd. #1502
Los Angeles, CA 90028

Brigitte Fossey
18 rue Troyon
75017, Paris, FRANCE

Jodie Foster
P.O. Box 846
Woodland Hills, CA 91367

Steve Franken
3604 Whitespeak Drive
Sherman Oaks, CA 91403

Meg Foster
9301 Wilshire Blvd. #312
Beverly Hills, CA 90210

Bonnie Franklin
14011 Ventura Blvd. #4018
Sherman Oaks, CA 91423

Susanna Foster
12255-F Morrison Street
North Hollywoood, CA 91601

Pamela Franklin
1280 Sunset Plaza Drive
Los Angeles, CA 90069

Michael J. Fox
3960 Laurel Canyon #281
Studio City, CA 91604

Mary Frann
151 South El Camino
Beverly Hills, CA 90212

Robert Foxworth
1230 Benedict Canyon Drive
Beverly Hills, CA 90210

Bert Freed
418 N. Bowling Green
Los Angeles, CA 90049

Redd Foxx
5676 S. Eastern Avenue
Las Vegas, NV 89119

Mona Freeman
608 N. Alpine Drive
Beverly Hills, CA 90210

Tony Franciosa
567 Tigertail Road
Los Angeles, CA 90049

Morgan Freeman
645 West End Avenue
New York, NY 10025

Anne Francis
P.O. Box 5417
Santa Barbara, CA 93103

Jourdan Fremin
128 1/2 N. Hamilton Drive
Beverly Hills, CA 90211

Genie Francis
5062 Calvin Avenue
Tarzana, CA 91356

Matt Frewer
5007 Roma Court
Marina del Rey, CA 90292

Joanna Frank
1274 Capri Drive
Pacific Palisades, CA 90272

Jonathan Frid
157 E. 18th Street #5-J
New York, NY 10003

Sonya Friedman
208 Harristown Road
Glen Rock, NJ 07452

Dan Frischman
717 N. Ontario Street
Burbank, CA 91505

David Frost
130 W. 57th Street
New York, NY 10019

Robert Fuller
8485-E Melrose Place
Los Angeles, CA 90069

Annette Funicello
16102 Sandy Lane
Encino, CA 91316

Stephen Furst
3900 Huntercrest Court
Moorpark, CA 93021

G   G

Eva Gabor
100 Delfern Drive
Los Angeles, CA 90077

Princess Zsa Zsa Gabor
1001 Bel Air Road
Los Angeles, CA 90077

Max Gail
29451 Bluewater
Malibu, CA 90265

Peter Gallagher
151 S. El Camino Drive
Beverly Hills, CA 90212

Teresa Ganzel
9744 Wilshire Blvd. #308
Beverly Hills, CA 90212

Andy Garcia
4519 Varna Avenue
Sherman Oaks, CA 91423

Vincent Gardenia
888 - 7th Avenue #2500
New York, NY 10106

James Garner
33 Oakmont Drive
Los Angeles, CA 90049

Teri Garr
1462 Rising Glen
Los Angeles, CA 90069

Betty Garrett
3231 Oakdell Road
Studio City, CA 91604

Greer Garson (Fogelson)
2400 Republic Bank Tower #11
Dallas, TX 75201

Mitch Gaylord
100 N. Woodburn Drive
Los Angeles, CA 90049

Lynda Day George
10310 Riverside Drive #104
Toluca Lake, CA 91602

Susan George
1221 N. Kings Road #104
Los Angeles, CA 90069

Richard Gere
45 E. 9th Street #98
New York, NY 10003

Estelle Getty
1140 N. Alta Loma Road #105
Los Angeles, CA 90069

Cynthia Gibb
151 S. El Camino Drive
Beverly, Hills, CA 90212

Leeza Gibbons
5555 Melrose Avenue #L
Los Angeles, CA 90038

Marla Gibbs
2323 W. King Blvd.
Los Angeles, CA 90008

Charles Gibson
1965 Broadway #500
New York, NY 10023

Mel Gibson
P.O. Box 2156
Santa Monica, CA 90406

Melissa Gilbert
337 W. 12th Street
New York, NY 10014

Erica Gimpel
888 - 7th Avenue #201
New York, NY 10019

Robin Givens
8818 Thrasher Avenue
Los Angeles, CA 90069

Paul Michael Glaser
317 Georgina Avenue
Santa Monica, CA 90402

Ron Glass
2485 Wild Oak Drive
Los Angeles, CA 90068

Scott Glenn
126 E. DeVargas Street, #1902
Santa Fe, NM 87501

Sharon Gless
4709 Teesdale Avenue
Studio City, CA 91604

Danny Glover
P.O. Box 590237
San Francisco, CA 94159

Jean-Luc Godard
15 rue du Nord
1180 Roulle,SWITZERLAND

Tracey Gold
12631 Addison Street
North Hollywood, CA 91607

Whoopi Goldberg
33012 Pacific Coast Hwy.
Malibu, CA 90265

Star Guide 1992-1993

Jeff Goldblum
8033 Sunset Blvd. #367
Los Angeles, CA 90046

Frank Gorshin
75 S. Morningside Drive
Westport, CT 06880

Louis Gossett, Jr.
P.O. Box 6187
Malibu, CA 90265

Elliott Gould
21250 Califa #201
Woodland Hills, CA 91367

Faye Grant
322 W. 20th Street
New York, NY 10011

Peter Graves
660 E. Channel Road
Santa Monica, CA 90402

Erin Gray
10921 Alta View
Studio City, CA 91604

Linda Gray
9255 Sunset Blvd. #716
Los Angeles, CA 90069

Michele Greene
2281 Holly Drive
Los Angeles, CA 90068

Jennifer Grey
27 Bethune Street
New York, NY 10014

Richard Grieco
15263 Mulholland Drive
Los Angeles, CA 90077

Pam Grier
6767 Hayvenhurst Avenue #315
Van Nuys, CA 91406

Andy Griffith
10500 Camarillo
North Hollywood, CA 91602

Melanie Griffith
9555 Heather Road
Beverly Hills, CA 90210

Sam Groom
140 Riverside Drive #16-0
New York, NY 10024

Michael Gross
521 Inverness Drive
La Canada, CA 91011

Christopher Guest
1242 S. Camden Drive
Los Angeles, CA 90035

Robert Guillaume
3853 Longridge Avenue
Sherman Oaks, CA 91423

Sir Alec Guiness
Kettle Brook Meadows
Petersfield, Hampshire, ENGLAND

Bryant Gumbel
30 Rockefeller Plaza #304
New York, NY 10020

29

Steve Guttenberg
15237 Sunset Blvd. #48
Pacific Palisades, CA 90272

Jasmine Guy
21243 Ventura Blvd. #101
Woodland Hills, CA 91364

H   H

Shelly Hack
1208 Georgina
Santa Monica, CA 90402

Gene Hackman
8500 Wilshire Blvd. #801
Beverly Hills, CA 90211

Uta Hagen
27 Washington Sq. North
New York, NY 10011

Larry Hagman
23730 Malibu Colony Road
Malibu, CA 90265

Charles Haid
4376 Forman Avenue
North Hollywood, CA 91602

Corey Haim
3960 Laurel Canyon Blvd. #384
Studio City, CA 91604

Anthony Michael Hall
65 Roosevelt Avenue
Valley Stream, NY 11581

Arsenio Hall
10987 Bluffside Drive #4108
Studio City, CA 91604

Monty Hall
519 N. Arden Drive
Beverly Hills, CA 90210

Veronica Hamel
2121 Avenue of the Stars #900
Los Angeles, CA 90067

Mark Hamill
9000 Sunset Blvd. #1200
Los Angeles, CA 90069

George Hamilton
9141 Burton Way #3
Beverly Hills, CA 90210

Linda Hamilton
8955 Norman Place
Los Angeles, CA 90069

Harry Hamlin
P.O. Box 25578
Los Angeles, CA 90025

Tom Hanks
321 S. Anita Avenue
Los Angeles, CA 90049

Daryl Hannah
151 El Camino Drive
Beverly Hills, CA 90212

Kadeem Hardison
324 N. Brighton Street
Burbank, CA 91506

Mariska Hargitay
9274 Warbler Way
Los Angeles, CA 90069

Mark Harmon
2236 Encinitas Blvd. #A
Encinitas, CA 92024

Tess Harper
2271 Betty Lane
Beverly Hills, CA 90210

Valerie Harper
616 N. Maple Drive
Beverly Hills, CA 90210

Woody Harrelson
1642 Westwood Blvd. #3
Los Angeles, CA 90024

Julie Harris
132 Barn Hill Road
West Chatham, MA 02669

Mel Harris
14755 Ventura Blvd. #1-904
Sherman Oaks, CA 91403

Richard Harris
630 Fifth Avenue #1510
New York, NY 10010

Jenilee Harrison
3800 Barham Blvd. #303
Los Angeles, CA 90068

Kathryn Harrold
151 S. El Camino Drive
Beverly Hills, CA 90212

Mary Hart
P.O. Box 1832
Los Angeles, CA 90078

Mariette Hartley
10100 Santa Monica Blvd. #2460
Los Angeles, CA 90067

Lisa Hartman
8037 Sunset Blvd. #2641
Los Angeles, CA 90046

David Hasselhoff
4310 Sutton Place
Van Nuys, CA 91403

Rutger Hauer
9255 Sunset Blvd. #505
Los Angeles, CA 90069

Wings Hauser
9113 Sunset Blvd.
Los Angeles, CA 90069

Goldie Hawn
1849 Sawtelle Blvd. #500
Los Angeles, CA 90025

Helen Hayes
235 N. Broadway
Nyack, NY 10960

Peter Lind Hayes
3538 Pueblo Way
Las Vegas, NV 89109

Tippi Hedren
1006 Fallen Leaf Road
Arcadia, CA 91006

Margaux Hemingway
151 El Camino
Beverly Hills, CA 90212

Mariel Hemingway
P.O. Box 2249
Ketchum, ID 83340

Shirley Hemphill
539 Trona Avenue
West Covina, CA 91790

Sherman Hemsley
8033 Sunset Blvd. #193
Los Angeles, CA 90046

Marilu Henner
2101 Castilian
Los Angeles, CA 90068

Audry Hepburn
Chalet Rico Bissenstrasse
Gstaad, SWITZERLAND

Katherine Hepburn
244 E. 49th Street
New York, NY 10017

Pee Wee Herman
12725 Ventura Blvd. #H
Studio City, CA 91604

Barbara Hershey
9830 Wilshire Blvd.
Beverly Hills, CA 90212

Howard Hesseman
7146 La Presa
Los Angeles, CA 90068

Charlton Heston
2859 Coldwater Canyon
Beverly Hills, CA 90210

Christopher Hewitt
10390 Santa Monica Blvd. #310
Los Angeles, CA 90025

Dwayne Hickman
812 - 16th Street #1
Santa Monica, CA 90403

Catherine Hicks
639 N. Larchmont Blvd. #207
Los Angeles, CA 90004

Gregory Hines
377 W. 11th Street, PH
New York, NY 10014

Judd Hirsch
P.O. Box 25909
Los Angeles, CA 90025

Dustin Hoffman
31045 Broad Beach Road
Malibu, CA 90265

Paul Hogan
1109 Tower Road
Beverly Hills, CA 90210

Hal Holbrook
618 S. Lucerne Blvd.
Los Angeles, CA 90005

Polly Holliday
888 - 7th Avenue #2500
New York, NY 10106

Celeste Holme
88 Central Park West
New York, NY 10023

Robert Hooks
145 N. Valley Street
Burbank, CA 91505

Bob Hope
10346 Moorpark
North Hollywood, CA 91602

Anthony Hopkins
7 High Park Road
Kew, Surrey,
Richmond, TW9 3BL, ENGLAND

Dennis Hopper
330 Indiana Avenue
Venice, CA 90291

Lee Horsley
1941 Cummings Drive
Los Angeles, CA 90027

Ken Howard
59 E. 54th Street
New York, NY 10022

Ron Howard
P.O. Box 299
Cos Cob, CT 06807

C. Thomas Howell
926 N. La Jolla Avenue
Los Angeles, CA 90046

Sally Ann Howes
19 W. 44th Street #1500
New York, NY 10036

Season Hubley
2645 Outpost Drive
Los Angeles, CA 90068

Leann Hunley
1888 N. Crecsent Heights
Los Angeles, CA 90069

Helen Hunt
3808 Fairway
Studio City, CA 91604

Linda Hunt
2593 N. Beachwood Drive
Los Angeles, CA 90068

Holly Hunter
9169 Sunset Blvd.
Los Angeles, CA 90069

Tab Hunter
Box 1048, La Tierra Nueva
Santa Fe, NM 87501

William Hurt
RD #1 - Box 251A
Palisades, NY 10964

Anjelica Huston
2771 Hutton Drive
Beverly Hills, CA 90210

Will Hutchins
3461 Waverly Drive #108
Los Angeles, CA 90027

Betty Hutton
Harrison Avenue
Newport, RI 02840

Lauren Hutton
54 Bond Street
New York, NY 10012

I   I

John Ireland
P.O. Box 5211
Santa Barbara, CA 93101

Amy Irving
11693 San Vicente Blvd. #335
Los Angeles, CA 90049

Jeremy Irons
194 Old Brompton Road
London, SW5, ENGLAND

Burl Ives
5012 Doon Way
Anacortes, WA 98221

Michael Ironside
10100 Santa Monica Blvd. #1600
Los Angeles, CA 90067

Judith Ivey
40 West 57th Street
New York, NY 10019

J   J

Jackee
8649 Metz Place
Los Angeles, CA 90069

Mary Ann Jackson
1242 Alessandro Drive
Newbury Park, CA 91320

Anne Jackson
90 Riverside Drive
New York, NY 10024

Paul Jackson Jr.
888 - 7th Avenue #1602
New York, NY 10019

Glenda Jackson
51 Harvey Road Blackheath
London, SE3, ENGLAND

Sherry Jackson
4933 Encino Avenue
Encino, CA 91316

Kate Jackson
1628 Marlay Drive
Los Angeles, CA 90069

Stoney Jackson
3151 Cahuenga Blvd. W. #310
Los Angeles, CA 90068

Victoria Jackson
8330 Lookout Mountain
Los Angeles, CA 90046

Derek Jacobi
22 Chelsham Road
London, SW4, ENGLAND

Lou Jacobi
240 Cantral Park South
New York, NY 10019

Scott Jacoby
1006 N. Edinburgh
Los Angeles, CA 90046

Richard Jaeckel
P.O. Box 1818
Santa Monica, CA 90406

John James
7310 Mulholland Drive
Los Angeles, CA 90046

Conrad Janis
1434 N. Genesee Avenue
Los Angeles, CA 90069

Lois January
225 N. Crescent Drive #103
Beverly Hills, CA 90210

Claude Jarman, Jr.
11 Dos Encinas
Orinda, CA 94563

Gabe Jarret
6640 Sunset Blvd. #203
Los Angeles, CA 90028

Graham Jarvis
15351 Via de las Olas
Pacific Palisades, CA 90272

Sybil Jason
345 S. Elm Drive #208
Beverly Hills, CA 90212

Gloria Jean
20309 Leadwell
Canoga Park, CA 91303

Zizi Jeanmaire
22 rue de la Paix
75002 Paris, FRANCE

Anne Jeffreys
121 S. Bentley Avenue
Los Angeles, CA 90049

Peter Jennings
47 West 66th Street
New York, NY 10023

Salome Jens
9400 Readcrest Drive
Beverly Hills, CA 90210

Ann Jillian
4141 Woodcliff Road
Sherman Oaks, CA 91403

Zita Johann
P.O. Box 302
West Nyack, NY 10994

Glynis Johns
6363 Wilshire Blvd. #600
Los Angeles, CA 90048

Anne-Marie Johnson
2606 Ivan Hill Terrace
Los Angeles, CA 90026

Arte Johnson
2725 Bottlebrush Drive
Los Angeles, CA 90024

Don Johnson
9555 Heather Road
Beverly Hills, CA 90210

Jill Johnson
43 Matheson Road
London, W14, ENGLAND

Laura Johnson
1917 Weepah Way
Los Angeles, CA 90046

Lynn-Holly Johnson
335 N. Maple Drive #250
Beverly Hills, CA 90210

Michelle Johnson
10351 Santa Monica Blvd. #211
Los Angeles, CA 90025

Rafer Johnson
4217 Woodcliff Road
Sherman Oaks, CA 91403

Russell Johnson
6310 San Vicente Blvd. #407
Los Angeles, CA 90048

Van Johnson
405 E. 54th Street
New York, NY 10022

Allan Jones
10 W. 66th Street
New York, NY 10023

Dean Jones
5055 Casa Drive
Tarzana, CA 91356

Gemma Jones
3 Goodwins Court
London, WC2, ENGLAND

Grace Jones
166 Bank Street
New York, NY 10014

James Earl Jones
14231 Valley Vista
Sherman Oaks, CA 91423

Janet Jones
4600 Balboa Blvd.
Encino, CA 91316

Jennifer Jones-Simon
P.O. Box 2248
Beverly Hills, CA 90213

Marcia Mae Jones
4541 Hazeltine Avenue #4
Sherman Oaks, CA 91423

Shirley Jones
701 N. Oakhurst Drive
Beverly Hills, CA 90210

Tommy Lee Jones
P.O. Box 966
San Saba, TX 76877

James Carroll Jordan
8333 Lookout Mountain
Los Angeles, CA 90046

Richard Jordan
3704 Carbon Canyon
Malibu, CA 90265

William Jordan
10806 Lindbrook Avenue #4
Los Angeles, CA 90024

Jackie Joseph
111 North Valley
Burbank, CA 91505

Louis Jourdan
1139 Maybrook
Beverly Hills, CA 90210

Elaine Joyce
724 N. Roxbury Drive
Beverly Hills, CA 90210

Raul Julia
200 W. 54th Street #7G
New York, NY 10019

Gordon Jump
1631 Hillcrest Avenue
Glendale, CA 91202

K   K

Madeline Kahn
975 Park Avenue #9A
New York, NY 10028

Helena Kallianotes
12830 Mulholland Drive
Beverly Hills, CA 90210

Steven Kampmann
812 Jacon Way
Pacific Palisades, CA 90272

Steve Kanaly
3611 Longridge Avenue
Sherman Oaks, CA 91423

Carol Kane
1416 N. Havenhurst Drive #1C
Los Angeles, CA 90046

Stan Kann
570 N. Rossmore Avenue
Los Angeles, CA 90004

Gabriel Kaplan
9551 Hidden Valley Road
Beverly Hills, CA 90210

Marvin Kaplan
1418 N. Highland Avenue #102
Los Angeles, CA 90028

James Karen
4455 Los Feliz Blvd. #807
Los Angeles, CA 90027

John Karlen
428 E. Lorraine
Glendale, CA 91207

Alex Karras
7943 Woodrow Wilson Drive
Los Angeles, CA 90046

Jean Kasem
138 N. Mapleton Drive
Los Angeles, CA 90077

William Katt
25218 Malibu Road
Malibu, CA 90265

Dianne Kay
1559 Palisades Drive
Pacific Palisades, CA 90272

Caren Kaye
217 - 16th Street
Santa Monica, CA 90402

James Keach
9229 Sunset Blvd. #607
Los Angeles, CA 90069

Stacy Keach, Jr.
27525 Winding Way
Malibu, CA 90265

Jane Kean
4332 Coldwater Canyon
Studio City, CA 91604

Diane Keaton
2255 Verde Oak Drive
Los Angeles, CA 90068

Michael Keaton
9830 Wilshire Blvd.
Beverly Hills, CA 90212

Lila Kedrova
162 Bd. Montparnasse
14 Paris, FRANCE

Don Keefer
4146 Allott Avenue
Sherman Oaks, CA 91403

Howard Keel
15353 Longbow Drive
Sherman Oaks, CA 91403

Ruby Keeler-Lowe
71029 Early Times Road
Rancho Mirage, CA 92270

Bob Keeshan
40 W. 57th Street #1600
New York, NY 10019

Harvey Keitel
110 Hudson Street #9A
New York, NY 10013

Brian Keith
23449 Malibu Colony Road
Malibu, CA 90265

David Keith
Chateau Marmont
8221 Sunset Blvd.
Los Angeles, CA 90069

Penelope Keith
66 Berkeley House
Hay Hill
London, SW3, ENGLAND

Martha Keller
5 rue St. Dominique
75007 Paris, FRANCE

Sally Kellerman
7944 Woodrow Wilson Drive
Los Angeles, CA 90046

De Forrest Kelley
15463 Greenleaf Street
Sherman Oaks, CA 91403

Gene Kelly
725 N. Rodeo Drive
Beverly Hills, CA 90210

Jack Kelly
P.O. Box 31
Huntington Beach, CA 92648

Paula Kelly
1801 Avenue of the Stars #1250
Los Angeles, CA 90067

Roz Kelly
5614 Lemp Avenue
North Hollywood, CA 91601

Linda Kelsey
1999 Avenue of the Stars #2850
Los Angeles, CA 90067

George Kennedy
1900 Ave, of the Stars #2270
Los Angeles, CA 90067

Jayne Kennedy
944 - 17th Street #1
Santa Monica, CA 90403

Mimi Kennedy
10100 Santa Monica Blvd. #1600
Los Angeles, CA 90067

Ken Kercheval
P.O. Box 1350
Los Angeles, CA 90078

Joanna Kerns
10100 Santa Monica Blvd. #1600
Los Angeles, CA 90067

Sandra Kerns
620 Resolano Drive
Pacific Palisades, CA 90272

Deborah Kerr
Los Monteros
E-29600 Marbella
Malaga, SPAIN

Linda Kerridge
9812 W. Olympic Blvd.
Beverly Hills, CA 90212

Brian Kerwin
10502 1/2 Wheatland Avenue
Sunland, CA 91040

Evelyn Keys
999 N. Doheny Drive
Los Angeles, CA 90069

Mark Keyloun
9255 Sunset Blvd. #505
Los Angeles, CA 90069

Persis Khambatta
113 N. San Vicente #202
Beverly Hills, CA 90011

Margot Kidder
7319 Beverly Blvd. #7
Los Angeles, CA 90036

Kaleena Kiff
6640 Sunset Blvd. #203
Los Angeles, CA 90028

Richard Kiley
Ryerson Road
Warwick Road, NY 10990

Lincoln Kilpatrick
12834 McLennan Avenue
Granada Hills, CA 91344

Roslyn Kind
8871 Burton Way #303
Los Angeles, CA 90048

Alan King
888 - 7th Avenue #3800
New York, NY 10106

Andrea King
1225 Sunset Plaza Drive #3
Los Angeles, CA 90069

Larry King
111 Massachusetts, NW 3rd Floor
Washington, DC 20001

Perry King
3747 Wrightwood Drive
Studio City, CA 91604

Ben Kingsley
Penworth, Stratford Upon Avon
Warwickshire, OV3 7QX,
ENGLAND

Klaus Kinski
33 Avenue Marshall Foch
F-75016 Paris, FRANCE

Nastassja Kinski
2121 Avenue of the Stars #990
Los Angeles, CA 90067

Durward Kirby
Rt. 37, Box 374
Sherman, CT 06734

Phyllis Kirk-Bush
11687 Bellagio Road #3
Los Angeles, CA 90049

Sally Kirkland
1930 Ocean Avenue
Santa Monica, CA 90405

Terry Kiser
5750 Wilshire Blvd. #512
Los Angeles, CA 90036

Tawny Kitaen
9255 Doheny Road #2501
Los Angeles, CA 90069

Eartha Kitt
1524 Labaig Avenue
Los Angeles, CA 90028

Werner Klemperer
44 W. 62nd Street, 10th Floor
New York, NY 10023

Kevin Kline
136 E. 57th Street #1001
New York, NY 10022

Richard Kline
14322 Mulholland Drive
Los Angeles, CA 90077

Jack Klugman
22548 Pacific Coast Hwy.
Malibu, CA 90265

Michael E. Knight
15760 Ventura Blvd. #1730
Encino, CA 91436

Shirley Knight
24 Mailmains Way
Beckenham, Kent, ENGLAND

Don Knotts
1854 S. Beverly Glen #402
Los Angeles, CA 90025

Walter Koenig
P.O. Box 4395
North Hollywood, CA 91607

Bernie Kopell
19413 Olivos
Tarzana, CA 91356

Ted Koppel
1717 DeSales N.W. #300
Washington, DC 20036

Harvey Korman
1136 Stradella Road
Los Angeles, CA 90077

Yaphet Kotto
1930 Century Park West #303
Los Angeles, CA 90067

Linda Kozlowski
1109 Tower Road
Beverly Hills, CA 90210

Stepfanie Kramer
8455 Beverly Blvd. #505
Los Angeles, CA 90048

Sylvia Kristal
8955 Norma Place
Los Angeles, CA 90069

L   L

Mathew Laborteaux
15301 Ventura Blvd. #345
Sherman Oaks, CA 91405

Patrick Laborteaux
1450 Belfast Drive
Los Angeles, CA 90069

Alan Ladd,
1420 Moraga Drive
Los Angeles, CA 90049

Cheryl Ladd
2485 Janin Way
Solvang, CA 93463

Diane Ladd
8440 DeLongpre Avenue #203
Los Angeles, CA 90069

Christine Lahti
10 W. 86th Street
New York, NY 10024

Hedy Lamarr
7915 East Drive #2L
Miami, FL 33141

Lorenzo Lamas
641 S. Mariposa Drive
Burbank, CA 91506

Dorothy Lamour
5309 Goodland Avenue
North Hollywood, CA 91607

Burt Lancaster
P.O. Box 67-B-38
Los Angeles, CA 90067

Martin Landau
9830 Wilshire Blvd.
Beverly Hills, CA 90212

Audrey Landers
1913 N. Beverly Drive
Beverly Hills, CA 90210

Judy Landers
9849 Denbigh
Beverly Hills, CA 90210

Steve Landesberg
355 N. Genesee Avenue
Los Angeles, CA 90036

Priscilla Lane
R.R. #1, N. Shore Road
Derry, NH 03038

SueAne Langdon
12725-C Ventura Blvd.
Studio City, CA 91604

Hope Lange
803 Bramble
Los Angeles, CA 90049

Jessica Lange
9830 Wilshire Blvd.
Beverly Hills, CA 90212

Ted Lange
19305 Redwing Street
Tarzana, CA 91356

Frank Langella
2121 Avenue of the Stars #950
Los Angeles, CA 90067

Angela Lansbury
635 Bonhill Road
Los Angeles, CA 90049

John Larroquette
P.O. Box 6303
Malibu, CA 90265

Jack Larson
449 Skyewiay Road North
Los Angeles, CA 90049

Dan Laurie
1420 N. Alta Vista
Los Angeles, CA 90046

John Phillip Law
1339 Miller Drive
Los Angeles, CA 90069

Carol Lawrence
12337 Ridge Circle
Los Angeles, CA 90049

Star Guide 1992-1993 TV/Movies

Steve Lawrence
820 Greenway Drive
Beverly Hills, CA 90210

Vicki Lawrence
6000 Lido Avenue
Long Beach, CA 90803

Robin Leach
875 - 3rd Avenue #1800
New York, NY 10022

Cloris Leachman
13127 Boca De Canon Lane
Los Angeles, CA 90049

Michael Learned
145 Central Park West
New York, NY 10023

Sabrina LeBeauf
133 St. Nichols Avenue
Englewood, NJ 07632

Kelly LeBrock
P.O. Box 727
Los Olivas, CA 93441

Christopher Lee
5 Sandown House
Wheat Field Terrace
London, W4, ENGLAND

Peggy Lee
2331 Century Hill
Los Angeles, CA 90067

Janet Leigh
1625 Summitridge Drive
Beverly Hills, CA 90210

Jennifer Jason Leigh
8531 Rosewood
Los Angeles, CA 90048

Chris Lemmon
7787 Hillside Avenue
Los Angeles, CA 90046

Jack Lemmon
141 S. El Camino Drive #201
Beverly Hills, CA 90212

Jay Leno
9000 Sunset Blvd. #400
Los Angeles, CA 90069

Rula Lenska
19 London Street
London, W2, ENGLAND

David Letterman
30 Rockefeller Plaza #1310 W
New York, NY 10020

Dawnn Lewis
9229 Sunset Blvd. #607
Los Angeles, CA 90069

Jerry Lewis
1701 Waldman Avenue
Las Vegas, NV 89102

Shari Lewis
603 N. Alta Drive
Beverly Hills, CA 90210

Judith Light
3410 Wrightview Drive
Studio City, CA 91604

Hal Linden
9200 Sunset Blvd. #PH-20
Los Angeles, CA 90069

Audra Lindley
9229 Sunset Blvd. #607
Los Angeles, CA 90069

Art Linkletter
1100 Bel Air Road
Los Angeles, CA 90077

Ray Liotta
9830 Wilshire Blvd.
Beverly Hills, CA 90212

Peggy Lipton-Jones
15250 Ventura Blvd. #900
Sherman Oaks, CA 91403

John Lithgow
1319 Warnall Avenue
Los Angeles, CA 90024

Cleavon Little
4374 Ventura Canyon #4
Sherman Oaks, CA 91403

Rich Little
24800 Pacific Coast Hwy.
Malibu, CA 90265

Christopher Lloyd
742 N. Sycamore Avenue
Los Angeles, CA 90038

Norman Lloyd
1813 Old Ranch Road
Los Angeles, CA 90049

Sondra Locke
111 Stone Canyon Road
Los Angeles, CA 90077

June Lockhart
404 San Vicente Blvd. #208
Santa Monica, CA 90402

Heather Locklear
4970 Summit View Drive
Westlake Village, CA 91362

Robert Loggia
1718 Angelo Drive
Beverly Hills, CA 90210

Julie London
16074 Royal Oaks
Encino, CA 91436

Shelly Long
15237 Sunset Blvd.
Pacific Palisade, CA 90272

Traci Lords
3349 Cahuenga Blvd. W. #2B
Los Angeles, CA 90068

Sophia Loren
1151 Hidden Valley Road
Thousand Oaks, CA 91360

Tina Louise
310 E. 46th Street #18-T
New York, NY 10017

Linda Lovelace (Marciano)
120 Enterprise
Secaucus, NJ 07094

Rob Lowe
975 Hancock Avenue #226
Los Angeles, CA 90069

Myrna Loy
425 E. 63rd Street
New York, NY 10021

Susan Lucci
16 Carteret Place
Garden City, NY 11530

Lorna Luft
1901 Avenue of the Stars #1600
Los Angeles, CA 90067

Ida Lupino
11665 Weddington Street
North Hollywood, CA 91601

Peter Lupus
11375 Dona Lisa Drive
Studio City, CA 91604

Dorothy Lyman
5613 Valley Oak Drive
Los Angeles, CA 90068

Carol Lynley
P.O. Box 2190
Malibu, CA 90265

M   M

Ralph Macchio
451 Deerpark Avenue
Dix Hills, NY 11746

Andie MacDowell
8899 Beverly Blvd.
Los Angeles, CA 90048

Ali MacGraw
1679 Alta Mura Road
Pacific Palisades, CA 90272

Janet MacLachlan
1919 N. Taft Avenue
Los Angeles, CA 90068

Kyle MacLachlan
828 Venezia
Venice, CA 90291

Shirley MacLaine
25200 Old Malibu Road
Malibu, CA 90265

Gavin MacLeod
14680 Valley Vista
Sherman Oaks, CA 91403

Fred MacMurray
458 Halvern Drive
Los Angeles, CA 90049

Patrick MacNee
39 Guildford Park Road
Guildford, Surrey GUZ 5NA
ENGLAND

Guy Madison
35022 1/2 Avenue "H"
Yucaipa, CA 92399

Virginia Madsen
8730 Santa Monica Blvd. #I
Los Angeles, CA 90069

Debra Sue Maffett
2969 Passmore Drive
Los Angeles, CA 90068

Lee Majors
23826 Malibu Road
Malibu, CA 90265

Chris Makepeace
15 Cleveland Street
Toronto, Ontario CANADA

Kristina Malandro
1750 N. Beverly Drive
Beverly Hills, CA 90210

Karl Malden
1845 Mandeville Canyon
Los Angeles, CA 90049

Nick Mancuso
7160 Grasswood Avenue
Malibu, CA 90265

Howie Mandell
9744 Wilshire Blvd. #308
Beverly Hills, CA 90212

Dinah Manoff
P.O. Box 5617
Beverly Hills, CA 90210

Marla Maples
420 Madison Avenue #1400
New York, NY 10017

Ann-Margret (Smith)
2707 Benedict Canyon
Beverly Hills, CA 90210

E.G. Marshall
RFD #2, Bryan Lake Road
Mount Kisco, NY 10549

Penny Marshall
7150 La Presa
Los Angeles, CA 90068

Peter Marshall
16714 Oakview Drive
Encino, CA 91316

Dean Martin
613 N. Linden Drive
Beverly Hills, CA 90210

Dick Martin
11030 Chalon Road
Los Angeles, CA 90077

Jared Martin
15060 Ventura Blvd #350
Sherman Oaks, CA 91403

Pamela Sue Martin
P.O. Box 25578
Los Angeles, CA 90025

Steve Martin
P.O. Box 929
Beverly Hills, CA 90213

Wink Martindale
1650 Venteran Avenue #104
Los Angeles, CA 90024

A Martinez
6835 Wild Life Road
Malibu, CA 90265

Marsha Mason
1200 Turquesa Lane
Pacific Palisades, CA 90272

Tom Mason
853 - 7th Avenue #9A
New York, NY 10019

Mary Stuart Masterson
40 W. 57th Street
New York, NY 10019

Marcello Mastroianni
Avenue CAV
via Maria Adelaide 8
Rome, ITALY

Jerry Mathers
23965 Via Aranda
Valencia, CA 91355

Tim Matheson
1221 Stone Canyon Road
Los Angeles, CA 90077

Marlee Matlin
335 N. Maple Drive #270
Beverly Hills, CA 90210

Walter Matthau
1875 Century Park East #2200
Los Angeles, CA 90067

Victor Mature
P.O. Box 706
Rancho Santa Fe, CA 92067

Virginia Mayo
109 E. Ave. De Las Arboles
Thousand Oaks, CA 91360

David McCallum
10 E. 44th Street #700
New York, NY 10017

Andrew McCarthy
4708 Vesper Avenue
Sherman Oaks, CA 91403

Kevin McCarthy
28264 Rey de Copas Lane
Malibu, CA 90265

Leigh McCloskey
6032 Philip Avenue
Malibu, CA 90265

Doug McClure
14936 Stonesbore Place
Sherman Oaks, CA 91403

Roddy McDowell
3110 Brookdale Road
Studio City, CA 91604

Spanky McFarland
8500 Buckner Lane
Ft. Worth, TX 76100

Darren McGavin
470 Park Avenue
New York, NY 10022

Vonette McGee
9744 Wilshire Blvd. #308
Beverly Hills, CA 90212

47

Kelly McGillis
13428 Maxella Avenue #513
Marina del Rey, CA 90292

Patrick McGoohan
16808 Bollinger Drive
Pacific Palisdes, CA 90272

Elizabeth McGovern
17319 Magnolia Blvd.
Encino, CA 91316

Maureen McGovern
529 W. 42nd Street #7F
New York, NY 10036

Dorothy McGuire
121 Copley Place
Beverly Hills, CA 90210

Stephen McHattie
9229 Sunset Blvd. #607
Los Angeles, CA 90069

Michael McKean
3570 Willowcrest Avenue
Studio City, CA 91604

Nancy McKeon
P.O. Box 6778
Burbank, CA 91510

Philip McKeon
10201 W. Pico Blvd.
Building 54, #6
Los Angeles, CA 90035

Ed McMahon
9115 Hazen Drive
Beverly Hills, CA 90210

Kristy McNichol
P.O. Box 5813
Sherman Oaks, CA 91413

Butterfly McQueen
31 Hamilton Terrace #3
New York, NY 10031

Chad McQueen
6169 La Gloria
Malibu, CA 90265

Gerald McRaney
1290 Inverness
Pasadena, CA 91101

Audrey Meadows
350 Trousdale Place
Beverly Hills, CA 90210

Jayne Meadows (Allen)
16185 Woodvale Road
Encino, CA 91316

Burgess Meredith
25 Malibu Colony Road
Malibu, CA 90265

Lee Ann Meriwether
P.O. Box 402
Encino, CA 91316

Alyssa Milano
12952 Woodbridge
Studio City, CA 91604

Sarah Miles
7 Windmill Street
London, W1, ENGLAND

Ann Miller
618 N. Alta Drive
Beverly Hills, CA 90210

Jason Miller
10000 Santa Monica Blvd. #305
Los Angeles, CA 90067

Donna Mills
2260 Benedict Canyon Drive
Beverly Hills, CA 90210

Hayley Mills
81 High Street
Hampton, Middlesex, ENGLAND

Yvette Mimieux
500 Perugia Way
Los Angeles, CA 90077

Robert Mitchum
860 San Ysidro Road
Santa Barbara, CA 93108

Kim Miyori
121 N. San Vicente Blvd.
Beverly Hills, CA 90211

Matthew Modine
1632 N. Beverly Drive
Beverly Hills, CA 90210

Richard Moll
7561 W. 82nd Street
Playa del Rey, CA 90293

Ricardo Montalban
1423 Oriole Drive
Los Angeles, CA 90069

Elizabeth Montgomery
1230 Benedict Canyon
Beverly Hills, CA 90210

Lee Montgomery
351 N. Orange Drive
Los Angeles, CA 90036

Clayton Moore
4720 Parkolivo
Calabasas, CA 91302

Demi Moore
9830 Wilshire Blvd.
Beverly Hills, CA 90212

Dudley Moore
73 Market Street
Venice, CA 90291

Garry Moore
12 S. Caliboque Cay
Hilton Head Island, SC 29928

Mary Tyler Moore
927 Fifth Avenue
New York, NY 10021

Melba Moore
200 Central Park S. #8R
New York, NY 10019

Roger Moore
Chalet Fenil
Grund bei Staad, SWITZERLAND

Esai Morales
1147 S. Wooster Street
Los Angeles, CA 90035

Erin Moran
11075 Santa Monica Blvd. #150
Los Angeles, CA 90025

Rick Moranis
90 Riverside Drive #14E
New York, NY 10024

Rita Moreno
1620 Amalfi Drive
Pacific Palisades, CA 90272

Harry Morgan
13172 Boca De Canon Lane
Los Angeles, CA 90049

Jaye P. Morgan
22345 Pacific Coast Hwy.
Malibu, CA 90265

Cathy Moriarity
4139 Via Marina #901
Marina del Rey, CA 90292

Michael Moriarty
200 W. 58th Street #3B
New York, NY 10019

Noriyuki "Pat" Morita
6815 Willoughby
Los Angeles, CA 90038

Robert Morley
Fairmans, Wargrave
Berkshire, ENGLAND

Billy Moses
405 Sycamore Road
Santa Monica, CA 90402

Roger Mosley
3756 Prestwick Drive
Los Angeles, CA 90027

Bill Moyers
524 W. 57th Street
New York, NY 10019

Kate Mulgrew
11938 Foxboro Drive
Los Angeles, CA 90049

Martin Mull
338 Chadbourne Avenue
Los Angeles, CA 90049

Greg Mullavey
4444 Hayvenhurst Avenue
Encino, CA 91436

Richard Mulligan
145 S. Beachwood Drive
Los Angeles, CA 90004

Ben Murphy
3601 Vista Pacifica #17
Malibu, CA 90265

Eddie Murphy
2727 Benedict Canyon
Beverly Hills, CA 90210

Bill Murray
RFD #1, Box 250A
Washington Springs Road
Palisades, NY 10964

Don Murray
15301 Ventura Blvd. #345
Sherman Oaks, CA 91403

Jim Nabors
151 El Camino Drive
Beverly Hills, CA 90212

Jack Narz
1905 Beverly Place
Beverly Hills, CA 90210

Patricia Neal
P.O. Box 1043
Edgartown, MA 02539

Liam Neeson
1999 Avenue of the Stars #2850
Los Angeles, CA 90067

Sam Neill
55 Park Lane
London, W14 5RE, ENGLAND

Craig T. Nelson
9350 Wilshire Blvd. #324
Beverly Hills, CA 90212

Harriet Nelson
4179 Valley Meadow
Encino, CA 91316

Bob Newhart
420 Amapola Lane
Los Angeles, CA 90077

Paul Newman
1120 - 5th Avenue #1C
New York, NY 10128

Phyllis Newman
211 Central Park W. #19E
New York, NY 10024

Julie Newmar
243 Carmelina
Los Angeles, CA 90049

Dr. Haing S. Ngor
945 N. Veaudry Avenue
Los Angeles, CA 90045

Nichelle Nichols
23281 Leonora Drive
Woodland Hills, CA 91367

Jack Nicholson
15760 Ventura Blvd. #1730
Encino, CA 91436

Julia Nickson-Soul
2232 Moreno Drive
Los Angeles, CA 90039

Leslie Nielsen
1622 Viewmont Drive
Los Angeles, CA 90069

Leonard Nimoy
801 Stone Canyon Road
Los Angeles, CA 90077

Philippi Noiret
104 rue des Sablons
F-78750 Mareil-Marly FRANCE

Nick Nolte
29555 Rainsford
Malibu, CA 90265

Deborah Norville
829 Park Avenue #10A
New York, NY 10021

Chuck Norris
18653 Ventura Blvd. #751
Tarzana, CA 91356

Michael Nouri
6036-C Hazelhurst Place
North Hollywood, CA 91606

Sheree North
27 Village Park Way
Santa Monica, CA 90405

Kim Novak
Rt. 3, Box 524
Carmel Highlands, CA 93921

O   O

Randi Oakes
3681 Alomar Drive
Sherman Oaks, CA 91423

Gary Oldham
235 Regent Street
London, W1, ENGLAND

Hugh O'Brian
3195 Benedict Canyon
Beverly Hills, CA 90210

Ken Olin
11840 Chaparal Street
Los Angeles, CA 90049

Carrol O'Connor
30826 Broadbeach Road
Malibu, CA 90265

Edward James Olmos
10000 Santa Monica Blvd. #305
Los Angeles, CA 90067

Donald O'Connor
P.O. Box 4524
North Hollywood, CA 91607

Patrick O'Neal
8428-C Melrose Place
Los Angeles, CA 90069

Maureen O'Hara
Box 1400, Christeansted
St. Croix, VI 00820

Ryan O'Neal
21368 Pacific Coast Hwy.
Malibu, CA 90265

Miles O'Keeffe
P.O. Box 216
Malibu, CA 90265

Tatum O'Neal
23712 Malibu Colony Road
Malibu, CA 90265

Jennifer O'Neil
32356 Mulholland Hwy.
Malibu, CA 90265

Ed O'Neill
2607 Grand Canal
Venice, CA 90291

Michael Ontkean
7120 Grasswood Avenue
Malibu, CA 90265

Bibi Osterwald
341 Carroll Park West
Long Beach, CA 90815

Maureen O'Sullivan
1839 Union Street
Schenectady, NY 12309

Annette O'Toole
360 Morton Street
Ashland, OR 97520

Peter O'Toole
98 Heath Street
London, NW3, ENGLAND

Catherine Oxenberg
P.O. Box 25909
Los Angeles, CA 90025

P   P

Jack Paar
9 Chateau Ridge Drive
Greenwich, CT 06830

Judy Pace
4139 Cloverdale
Los Angeles, CA 90008

Al Pacino
9 E. 68th Street #5B
New York, NY 10021

Janis Paige
1700 Rising Glen Road
Los Angeles, CA 90069

Holly Palance
2753 Roscomare Road
Los Angeles, CA 90077

Jack Palance
Star Rt. 1, Box 805
Tehachapi, CA 93561

Michael Pare
9019 Dorrington Avenue
Los Angeles, CA 90048

Eleanor Parker
2195 La Paz Way
Palm Spring, CA 92262

Fess Parker
P.O. Box 50440
Santa Barbara, CA 93150

Jamerson Parker
419 N. Larchmont Blvd. #288
Los Angeles, CA 90004

Sarah Jessica Parker
1494 N. Kings Road
Los Angeles, CA 90069

Barbara Parkins
1930 Century Park W. #403
Los Angeles, CA 90067

Bert Parks
Skyridge Road
Greenwich, CT 06830

Robert Pastorelli
2751 Holly Ridge Drive
Los Angeles, CA 90068

Mandy Patinkin
200 W. 90th Street
New York, NY 10024

Adrian Paul
9000 Sunset Blvd. #801
Los Angeles, CA 90069

Jane Pauley
271 Central Park W. #10E
New York, NY 10024

Gregory Peck
P.O. Box 837
Beverly Hills, CA 90213

Thaao Penghlis
10390 Santa Monica Blvd. #310
Los Angeles, CA 90025

Christopher Penn
6728 Zumirez Drive
Malibu, CA 90265

Sean Penn
P.O. Box 2630
Malibu, CA 90265

Joe Penny
10453 Sarah
North Hollywood, CA 91602

Sydney Penny
3090 Calvert Court
Camarillo, CA 93010

George Peppard
P.O. Box 1643
Beverly Hills, CA 90213

Tony Perkins
2840 Seattle Drive
Los Angeles, CA 90046

Ron Perlman
345 N. Maple Drive #183
Beverly Hills, CA 90210

Valerie Perrine
8271 Melrose Avenue #110
Los Angeles, CA 90046

Joe Pesci
9830 Wilshire Blvd. #1825
Beverly Hills, CA 90212

Donna Pescow
9285 Flicker Place
Los Angeles, CA 90069

Bernadette Peters
8651 Pine Tree Place
Los Angeles, CA 90069

Brock Peters
1420 Rising Glen Road
Los Angeles, CA 90069

Michelle Pfeiffer
3930 Legion Lane
Los Angeles, CA 90039

Julianne Phillips
10390 Santa Monica Blvd. #300
Los Angeles, CA 90025

Lou Diamond Phillips
2427 Castilian
Los Angeles, CA 90068

Mackenzie Phillips
13743 Victory Blvd.
Van Nuys, CA 91401

River Phoenix
P.O. Box 520
Royal Palm Beach, FL 33411

Cindy Pickett
2423 Green Valley Road
Los Angeles, CA 90046

Mary Kay Place
2739 Motor Avenue
Los Angeles, CA 90064

Dana Plato
6194 W. Flamingo
Las Vegas, NV 89103

Suzanne Pleshette
1100 Alta Loma Road
Los Angeles, CA 90069

Christopher Plummer
49 Wampum Hill Road
Weston, CT 06883

Sidney Poitier
1007 Cove Way
Beverly Hills, CA 90210

Markie Post
4425 Talofa
Toluca Lake, CA 91602

Annie Potts
1601 North Campbell
Glendale, CA 91207

Jane Powell
230 W. 55th Street #14B
New York, NY 10019

Stefanie Powers
2661 Hutton Drive
Beverly Hills, CA 90210

Paula Prentiss
719 N. Foothill Road
Beverly Hills, CA 90210

Priscilla Presley
1167 Summit Drive
Beverly Hills, CA 90210

Vincent Price
9255 Swallow Drive
Los Angeles, CA 90069

Jason Priestly
8961 Sunset Blvd. #2A
Los Angeles, CA 90069

William Prince
750 N. Kings Road #307
Los Angeles, CA 90069

Victoria Principal
9220 Sunset Blvd. #302
Los Angeles, CA 90069

Andrew Prine
3364 Longridge Avenue
Sherman Oaks, CA 91403

Juliet Prowse
343 S. Beverly Glen
Los Angeles, CA 90077

Richard Pryor
1115 Moraga Drive
Los Angeles, CA 90049

Keshia Knight Pulliam
P.O. Box 866
Teaneck, NJ 07666

Sarah Purcell
323 North Carmelina
Los Angeles, CA 90049

Linda Purl
P.O. Box 5617
Beverly Hills, CA 90210

Q   Q

Dennis Quaid
9830 Wilshire Blvd.
Beverly Hills, CA 90210

Randy Quaid
15760 Ventura Blvd. #1730
Encino, CA 91316

Linnea Quigley
12710 Blythe Street
N. Hollywood, CA 91605

Kathleen Quinlan
P.O. Box 2465
Malibu, CA 90265

Aidan Quinn
9830 Wilshire Blvd.
Beverly Hills, CA 90212

Anthony Quinn
2 E. 86th Street
New York, NY 10028

R   R

Deborah Raffin
2630 Eden Place
Beverly Hills, CA 90210

Dack Rambo
Rambo Horse Farm
Earlimart, CA 93219

Harold Ramis
14198 Alisal Lane
Santa Monica, CA 90402

Tony Randall
1 West 81st Street #6D
New York, NY 10024

Sally Jessy Raphael
510 W. 57th Street #200
New York, NY 10019

Phylicia Rashad
448 W. 44th Street
New York, NY 10036

Dan Rather
51 W. 52nd Street
New York, NY 10019

Martha Raye
1153 Roscomare Road
Los Angeles, CA 90077

Peter Reckell
8033 Sunset Blvd. #4016
Los Angeles, CA 90046

Robert Redford
Rt. 3, Box 837
Provo, UT 84601

Lynn Redgrave
21342 Colina Drive, Box 186
Topanga, CA 90290

Vanessa Redgrave
31/32 Soho Square
London, W1, ENGLAND

Shanna Reed
1649 South Sterns Drive
Los Angeles, CA 90035

Della Reese
1910 Bel Air Road
Los Angeles, CA 90077

Christopher Reeve
100 W. 78th Street #5A
New York, NY 10024

Keanu Reeves
7920 Sunset Blvd. #250
Los Angeles, CA 90046

Duncan Regehr
5319 Wilkinson Avenue
North Hollywood, CA 91607

Tim Reid
16030 Ventura Blvd. #380
Encino, CA 91436

Carl Reiner
714 N. Rodeo Drive
Beverly Hills, CA 90210

Rob Reiner
255 Chadbourne Avenue
Los Angeles, CA 90069

Judge Reinhold
1341 Ocean Avenue #113
Santa Monica, CA 90401

Paul Reiser
9255 Sunset Blvd. #716
Los Angeles, CA 90069

Burt Reynolds
1001 Indiantown Road
Jupiter, FL 33458

Debbie Reynolds
11595 La Maida
North Hollywood, CA 91602

Cynthia Rhodes
15250 Ventura Blvd. #900
Sherman Oaks, CA 91403

Don Rickles
925 N. Alpine Drive
Beverly Hills, CA 90210

Diana Rigg
235 Regent Street
London, W7, ENGLAND

Molly Ringwald
7680 Mulholland Drive
Los Angeles, CA 90046

John Ritter
236 Tigertail Road
Los Angeles, CA 90049

Geraldo Rivera
49 E. 96th Street PH, "A"
New York, NY 10128

Joan Rivers
555 W. 57th Street #900
New York, NY 10019

Jason Robards
888 - 7th Avenue #1800
New York, NY 10019

Eric Roberts
888 - 7th Avenue #1602
New York, NY 10019

Julia Roberts
955 S. Carrillo Drive #200
Los Angeles, CA 90048

Pernell Roberts
20395 Seaboard Road
Malibu, CA 90265

Tanya Roberts
10090 Cielo Drive
Beverly Hills, CA 90210

Tony Roberts
970 Park Avenue #8N
New York, NY 10028

Cliff Robertson
325 Dunemere Drive
La Jolla, CA 92037

Ginger Rogers
18745 Crater Lake, Highway 62
Eagle Point, OR 97524

Mimi Rogers
15226 1/2 Dickens Street
Sherman Oaks, CA 91403

Mr. Rogers (Fred)
4802 - 5th Avenue
Pittsburgh, PA 15213

Roy Rogers
15650 Seneca Road
Victorville, CA 92392

Tristan Rogers
151 El Camino Drive
Los Angeles, CA 90212

Wayne Rogers
11828 La Grange Avenue
Los Angeles, CA 90025

Roxie Roker
4061 Cloverdale Avenue
Los Angeles, CA 90008

Esther Rolle
P.O. Box 8986
Los Angeles, CA 90008

Howard E. Rollins, Jr.
123 W. 85th Street #4F
New York, NY 10024

Cesar Romero
12115 San Vicente Blvd. #302
Los Angeles, CA 90049

Andy Rooney
254 Rowayton Avenue
Rowayton, CT 06853

Mickey Rooney
4165 Thousand Oaks Blvd.
Westlake Village, CA 91362

Rosemarie
6916 Chisholm Avenue
Van Nuys, CA 91406

Katharine Ross
33050 Pacific Coast Hwy.
Malibu, CA 90265

Isabella Rossellini
260 W. Broadway #5B
New York, NY 10013

Richard Roundtree
8721 Sunset Blvd. #202
Los Angeles, CA 90069

Mickey Rourke
1778 Old Ranch Road
Los Angeles, CA 90049

Misty Rowe
9278 Warbler Way
Los Angeles, CA 90069

Gena Rowlands
7917 Woodrow Wilson Drive
Los Angeles, CA 90046

Jane Russell
2934 Lorito Road
Santa Barbara, CA 93108

Kimberly Russell
10231 Riverside Drive #203
Toluca Lake, CA 91602

Kurt Russell
229 E. Gainsborough Road
Thousand Oaks, CA 91360

Nipsey Russell
353 W. 57th Street
New York, NY 10019

Winona Ryder
722 Copeland Court #3
Santa Monica, CA 90405

S   S

Morely Safer
555 W. 57th Street
New York, NY 10019

Katey Sagal
3498 Troy Drive
Los Angeles, CA 90068

Bob Saget
9200 Sunset Blvd. #428
Los Angeles, CA 90069

Eva Marie Saint
8271 Melrose Avenue #110
Los Angeles, CA 90046

Susan Saint James
854 N. Genessee Avenue
Los Angeles, CA 90046

Jill St. John
1500 Old Oak Road
Los Angeles, CA 90077

Pat Sajak
3400 Riverside Drive
Burbank, CA 91505

Soupy Sales
245 E. 35th Street
New York, NY 10016

Emma Samms
P.O. Box 60257
Los Angeles, CA 90060

William Sanderson
469 North Croft
Los Angeles, CA 90069

Chris Sarandon
121 N. San Vicente Blvd.
Beverly Hills, CA 90211

Susan Sarandon
25 E. 9th Street
New York, NY 10019

Dick Sargent
7422 Palo Vista Drive
Los Angeles, CA 90046

Fred Savage
P.O. Box 893
Tarzana, CA 91357

Telly Savalas
8 Surrey Court
Rancho Mirage, CA 92270

Diane Sawyer
1965 Broadway #400
New York, NY 10023

John Saxon
2432 Banyan Drive
Los Angeles, CA 90049

Jack Scalia
2150 Cold Canyon
Calabasas, CA 91302

Star Guide 1992-1993   TV/Movies

William Schallert
14920 Ramos Place
Pacific Palisades, CA 90272

Roy Scheider
120 E. 56th Street #8N
New York, NY 10022

Daniel Schneider
12840 Moorpark #308
Studio City, CA 91604

John Schneider
P.O. Box 741
Pacific Palisades, CA 90272

Rick Schroder
921 N. Roxbury Drive
Beverly Hills, CA 90210

Arnold Schwarzenegger
321 Hampton Drive #203
Venice, CA 90291

Tracy Scoggins
P.O. Box 2262
Malibu, CA 90265

George C. Scott
3211 Retreat Court
Malibu, CA 90265

Lizabeth Scott
P.O. Box 5522
Beverly Hills, CA 90213

Willard Scott
30 Rockefeller Plaza #304
New York, NY 10012

George Segal
8899 Beverly Blvd.
Los Angeles, CA 90048

Connie Selleca
P.O. Box 60257
Los Angeles, CA 90060

Tom Selleck
4095 Black Point Road
Honolulu, HI 96815

Jane Seymour
St. Catherine's Court
Batheaston, Bath
Avon, ENGLAND

Ted Shackleford
12305 Valleyheart Drive
Studio City, CA 91604

Garry Shandling
9200 Sunset Blvd. #428
Los Angeles, CA 90069

Omar Sharif
31/32 Soho Square
London, W1, ENGLAND

Ray Sharkey
12424 Wilshire Blvd. #840
Los Angeles, CA 90025

William Shatner
3674 Berry Avenue
Studio City, CA 91604

Helen Shaver
10390 Santa Monica Blvd. #300
Los Angeles, CA 90025

Ally Sheedy
P.O. Box 6327
Malibu, CA 90264

Charlie Sheen
11770 Pacific Coast Hwy.
Malibu, CA 90265

Martin Sheen
6919 Dune Drive
Malibu, CA 90265

Deborah Shelton
1690 Coldwater Canyon
Beverly Hills, CA 90210

Cybill Shepherd
16037 Royal Oak Road
Encino, CA 91436

Sam Shepherd
240 W. 44th Street
New York, NY 10036

Nicholette Sheridan
P.O. Box 25578
Los Angeles, CA 90025

Brooke Shields
P.O. Box 147
Harrington Park, NJ 07640

Yoko Shimada
7245 Hillside Avenue #415
Los Angeles, CA 90046

Martin Short
15907 Alcima Avenue
Pacific Palisades, CA 90272

Kin Shriner
4664 W. Willis Avenue
Sherman Oaks, CA 91403

Wil Shriner
5313 Quakertown Avenue
Woodland Hills, CA 91364

Maria Shriver
321 Hampton Drive #203
Venice, CA 90291

Elizabeth Shue
217 Turell Avenue
South Orange, NJ 07079

Sylvia Sidney
9744 Wilshire Blvd. #308
Beverly Hills, CA 90212

Henry Silva
8747 Clifton Way #305
Beverly Hills, CA 90212

Jean Simmons
636 Adelaide Way
Santa Monica, CA 90402

Lori Singer
330 W. 72nd Street #10B
New York, NY 10023

Marc Singer
11218 Canton Drive
Studio City, CA 91604

Mirina Sirtis
2436 Creston Way
Los Angeles, CA 90068

Gene Siskel
1301 N. Astor
Chicago, IL 60610

Red Skelton
87801 Thompson Road
Rancho Mirage, CA 92270

Christian Slater
5871 Allott
Van Nuys, CA 91401

Helen Slater
151 S. El Camino Drive
Beverly Hills, CA 90212

Jean Smart
4545 Noeline Avenue
Encino, CA 91316

Alexis Smith
25 Central Park West
New York, NY 10023

Allison Smith
8899 Beverly Blvd.
Los Angeles, CA 90048

Buffalo Bob Smith
Big Lake
Princeton, ME 04619

Cotter Smith
14755 Ventura Blvd. #1-904
Sherman Oaks, CA 91403

Jaclyn Smith
773 Stradella Road
Los Angeles, CA 90077

Maggie Smith
388 - 396 Oxford Street
London, W1, ENGLAND

Jan Smithers
803 Country Club Drive
Ojai, CA 93023

Jimmy Smits
110 S. Westgate Avenue
Los Angeles, CA 90049

Dick Smothers
P. O. Box 1685
Soquel, CA 95073

Tom Smothers
8489 W. Third Street
Los Angeles, CA 90048

Carrie Snodgrass
3025 Surry Street
Los Angeles, CA 90027

Tom Snyder
2801 Hutton Drive
Beverly Hills, CA 90210

Suzanne Somers
190 N. Canon Drive #201
Beverly Hills, CA 90210

Elke Sommer
540 N. Beverly Glen
Los Angeles, CA 90024

David Soul
2232 Moreno Drive
Los Angeles, CA 90039

Sissy Spacek
9830 Wilshire Blvd.
Los Angeles, CA 90212

Andrew Stevens
9612 Arby Drive
Beverly Hills, CA 90210

James Spader
8899 Beverly Blvd.
Los Angeles, CA 90048

Stella Stevens
2180 Coldwater Canyon
Beverly Hills, CA 90210

Robert Stack
321 St. Pierre Road
Los Angeles, CA 90077

McLean Stevenson
P.O. Box 1668
Studio City, CA 91604

James Stacy
478 Severn Avenue
Tampa, FL 33606

Parker Stevenson
4875 Louise Avenue
Encino, CA 91316

Sylvester Stallone
9750 Wanda Park Drive
Beverly Hills, CA 90210

Catherine Mary Stewart
500 Beloit Avenue
Los Angeles, CA 90049

John Stamos
22139 Mulholland Drive
Woodland Hills, CA 91436

James Stewart
P.O. Box 90
Beverly Hills, CA 90213

Harry Dean Stanton
14527 Mulholland Drive
Los Angeles, CA 90077

Dean Stockwell
535 Concha Loma Drive
Carpinteria, CA 93013

Jean Stapleton
635 Perugia Way
Los Angeles, CA 90077

Guy Stockwell
4924 Cahuenga Blvd.
North Hollywood, CA 91601

Maureen Stapleton
1 Bolton Drive
Lenox, MA 01240

Eric Stoltz
2320 Vista Madera
Santa Barbara, CA 93101

David Steinberg
16121 High Valley Place
Encino, CA 91436

Sharon Stone
7808 Torreyson Drive
Los Angeles, CA 90046

Robin Strasser
9301 Wilshire Blvd. #312
Beverly Hills, CA 90210

Marcia Strassman
8756 Holloway Drive
Los Angeles, CA 90069

Peter Strauss
8899 Beverly Blvd.
Los Angeles, CA 90048

Meryl Streep
9830 Wilshire Blvd.
Beverly Hills, CA 90212

Sally Struthers
181 N. Saltair Avenue
Los Angeles, CA 90049

Donald Sutherland
760 N. La Cienega Blvd. #300
Los Angeles, CA 90069

Kiefer Sutherland
1033 Gayley Avenue #208
Los Angeles, CA 90024

Bo Svenson
801 Greentree Road
Pacific Palisades, CA 90272

Patrick Swayze
11420 Lemoncrest
Lakeview Terrace, CA 91342

Loretta Swit
24216 Malibu Road
Malibu, CA 90265

T   T

Mr. T
395 Green Bay Road
Lake Forest, IL 60045

George Takei
3800 Barham Blvd. #303
Los Angeles, CA 90068

Jessica Tandy
63 - 23 Carlton Street
Rego Park, NY 11374

Elizabeth Taylor
700 Nimes Road
Los Angeles, CA 90077

Leigh Taylor-Young
1279 Beverly Estate Drive
Beverly Hills, CA 90210

Rod Taylor
2375 Bowmont Drive
Beverly Hills, CA 90210

Deney Terrio
1541 N. Vine Street
Los Angeles, CA 90028

John Tesh
2400 Broadway #100
Santa Monica, CA 90404

Lauren Tewes
341 N. Beachwood Drive
Los Angeles, CA 90004

Brynn Thayer
9301 Wilshire Blvd. #312
Beverly Hills, CA 90210

Alan Thicke
10505 Sarah
Toluca Lake, CA 91602

Roy Thinnes
8016 Willow Glen Road
Los Angeles, CA 90046

Heather Thomas
1433 San Vicente Blvd.
Santa Monica, CA 90402

Henry Thomas
9200 Sunset Blvd. #710
Los Angeles, CA 90069

Marlo Thomas
420 E. 54th Street #22F
New York, NY 10022

Melody Thomas-Scott
20620 Kingsboro Way
Woodland Hills, CA 91364

Philip Michael Thomas
12615 W. Dixie Highway
North Miami, FL 33161

Richard Thomas
4834 Bonvue
Los Angeles, CA 90027

Lea Thompson
7966 Woodrow Wilson Drive
Los Angeles, CA 90046

Sada Thompson
P.O. Box 490
Southebury, CT 06488

Gordon Thomson
2515 Astral Drive
Los Angeles, CA 90046

Gene Tierney-Lee
2200 Willowick, #5A
Houston, TX 77027

Pamela Tiffin
15 W. 67th Street
New York, NY 10023

Meg Tilly
321 S. Beverly Drive #M
Beverly Hills, CA 90212

Charlene Tilton
4634 Azalia
Tarzana, CA 91356

Beverly Todd
4888 Valley Ridge
Los Angeles, CA 90043

Lily Tomlin
P.O. Box 27700
Los Angeles, CA 90027

Angel Tompkins
1930 Century Park West #303
Los Angeles, CA 90067

Rip Torn
130 W. 42nd Street #2400
New York, NY 10036

Fred Travalena
4515 White Oak Place
Encino, CA 91316

Daniel J. Travanti
14205 Sunset Blvd.
Pacific Palisades, CA 90272

John Travolta
1504 Live Oak Lane
Santa Barbara, CA 93105

Alex Trebek
7966 Mulholland Drive
Los Angeles, CA 90046

Kathleen Turner
130 W. 42nd Street
New York, NY 10036

Lana Turner
10101 Santa Monica Blvd. #700
Los Angeles, CA 90067

Shannon Tweed
9300 Wilshire Blvd. #410
Beverly Hills, CA 90210

Cicely Tyson
315 W. 70th Street
New York, NY 10023

Richard Tyson
10100 Santa Monica Blvd. #1600
Los Angeles, CA 90067

U   U

Leslie Uggams
9255 Sunset Blvd. #404
Los Angeles, CA 90069

Dr. Art Ulene
10810 Via Verona
Los Angeles, CA 90024

Liv Ullman
15 W. 81st Street
New York, NY 10024

Blair Underwood
7148 Woodrow Wilson Drive
Los Angeles, CA 90046

Robert Urich
15930 Woodvale Road
Encino, CA 91436

Bonnie Urseth
9229 Sunset Blvd. #306
Los Angeles, CA 90069

Peter Ustinov
11 Rue de Silly
92100, Boulogne, FRANCE

Garrick Utley
12 Hanover Terrace
London, W1, ENGLAND

V   V

Karen Valentine
145 W. 67th Street #42H
New York, NY 10023

Joan Van Ark
10950 Alta View Drive
Studio City, CA 91604

Jean-Claude Van Damme
P.O. Box 4149
Chatsworth, CA 91313

Mamie Van Doren
428 - 31st Street
Newport Beach, CA 92663

Dick Van Dyke
23215 Mariposa De Oro
Malibu, CA 90265

Jerry Van Dyke
1717 N. Highland Avenue #414
Los Angeles, CA 90028

Dick Van Patten
13920 Magnolia Blvd.
Sherman Oaks, CA 91423

Vincent Van Patten
13926 Magnolia Blvd.
Sherman Oaks, CA 91423

Robert Vaughn
162 Old West Mountain Road
Ridgefield, CT 06877

Abe Vigoda
1215 Beverly View Drive
Beverly Hills, CA 90210

Herve Villechaize
P.O. Box 1305
Burbank, CA 91507

Jan-Michael Vincent
P.O. Box 7000-690
Redondo Beach, CA 90277

Jon Voight
13340 Galewood Drive
Sherman Oaks, CA 91423

Max Von Sydow
C-G Risbery Strandvegen B
114-56, Stockholm, SWEDEN

W   W

Lyle Waggoner
4450 Balboa Avenue
Encino, CA 91316

Lindsay Wagner
P.O. Box 188
Pacific Palisades, CA 90272

Robert Wagner
10000 Santa Monica Blvd. #400
Los Angeles, CA 90067

Ken Wahl
6622 Portshead Drive
Malibu, CA 90265

Robert Walden
1450 Arroyo View Drive
Pasadena, CA 91103

Christopher Walken
142 Cedar Road
Wilton, CT 06897

Jimmy Walker
9000 Sunset Blvd. #400
Los Angeles, CA 90069

Marcy Walker
4573 Greenbush Avenue
Sherman Oaks, CA 91423

Nancy Walker
3702 Eureka
North Hollywood, CA 91602

Mike Wallace
555 W. 57th Street
New York, NY 10019

Barbara Walters
33 W. 60th Street
New York, NY 10021

Susan Walters
10100 Santa Monica Blvd. #1600
Los Angeles, CA 90067

Judge Joseph Wapner
16616 Park Lane Place
Los Angeles, CA 90049

Fred Ward
9301 Wilshire Blvd. #312
Beverly Hills, CA 90210

Sela Ward
2102 Century Park Lane #202
Los Angeles, CA 90067

Marsha Warfield
P.O. Box 691713
Los Angeles, CA 90069

Malcolm-Jamal Warner
1301 The Colony
Hartsdale, NY 10530

Lesley Ann Warren
3619 Meadville
Sherman Oaks, CA 91403

Denzel Washington
4701 Sancola
Toluca Lake, CA 91602

Keenan Ivory Wayans
451 N. Orange Drive
Los Angeles, CA 90036

Patrick Wayne
10502 Whipple Street
North Hollywood, CA 91602

Dennis Weaver
P.O. Box 983
Malibu, CA 90265

Sigourney Weaver
12 W. 72nd Street
New York, NY 10023

Steven Weber
151 S. El Camino Drive
Beverly Hills, CA 90212

Bruce Weitz
3061 Lake Hollywood Drive
Los Angeles, CA 90068

Raquel Welch
540 Evelyn Place
Beverly Hills, CA 90210

Tahnee Welch
200 Central Park South
New York, NY 10019

Tuesday Weld
300 Central Park W. #14E
New York, NY 10024

Peter Weller
853 - 7th Avenue #9A
New York, NY 10019

George Wendt
3856 Vantage Avenue
Studio City, CA 91604

Patricia Wettig
11840 Chaparal Street
Los Angeles, CA 90049

Wil Wheaton
2603 Seapine Lane
La Crescenta, CA 91214

Lisa Whelchel
11906 Shoshone Avenue
Granada Hills, CA 91344

Betty White
P.O. Box 3713
Granada Hills, CA 91344

Vanna White
3400 Riverside Drive
Burbank, CA 91505

Stuart Whitman
749 San Ysidro Road
Santa Barbara, CA 93108

James Whitmore
25 Central Park West
New York, NY 10023

Richard Widmark
999 W. Portrero Road
Thousand Oaks, CA 91360

Gene Wilder
9350 Wilshire Blvd. #400
Beverly Hills, CA 90210

Anson Williams
439 N. Doheny Drive #605
Beverly Hills, CA 90210

Billy Dee Williams
1240 Loma Vista Drive
Beverly Hills, CA 90210

Cindy Williams
7023 Birdview Avenue
Malibu, CA 90265

Esther Williams
9377 Readcrest Drive
Beverly Hills, CA 90210

Jobeth Williams
3529 Beverly Glen Blvd.
Sherman Oaks, CA 91423

Robin Williams
1100 Wall Road
Napa, CA 94550

Bruce Willis
1122 S. Robertson Blvd. #15
Los Angeles, CA 90035

Flip Wilson
21970 Pacific Coast Hwy.
Malibu, CA 90265

Paul Winfield
5693 Holly Oak Drive
Los Angeles, CA 90068

Oprah Winfrey
P.O. Box 909715
Chicago, IL 60690

Debra Winger
P.O. Box 1368
Pacific Palisades, CA 90272

Henry Winkler
4323 Forman Avenue
Toluca Lake, CA 91604

Jonathan Winters
4310 Arcola Avenue
Toluca Lake, CA 91602

Shelly Winters
457 N. Oakhurst Drive
Beverly Hills, CA 90210

James Woods
1612 Gilcrest Drive
Beverly Hills, CA 90210

Edward Woodward
10 E. 40th Styreet #2700
New York, NY 10016

Joanne Woodward
1120 - 5th Avenue #1C
New York, NY 10128

Tom Wopat
12245 Morrison Street
North Hollywood, CA 91607

Jane Wyman
P.O. Box 540148
Orlando, FL 32854

Y   Y

Amy Yasbeck
1309 Summertime Lane
Culver City, CA 90230

Michael York
9100 Cordell Drive
Los Angeles, CA 90069

Loretta Young
1705 Ambassador Drive
Beverly Hills, CA 90210

Sean Young
300 Mercer Street #7E
New York, NY 10003

Z   Z

Pia Zadora
8 Beverly Park
Beverly Hills, CA 90210

Efrem Zimbalist, Jr.
4750 Encino Avenue
Encino, CA 91316

Paula Zahn
524 West 57th Street
New York, NY 10019

Stephanie Zimbalist
153 S. Camden Drive
Beverly Hills, CA 90212

Roxana Zal
1450 Belfast Drive
Los Angeles, CA 90069

Kim Zimmer
9200 Sunset Blvd. #710
Los Angeles, CA 90069

Jacklyn Zeman
12186 Lauerel Terrace
Studio City, CA 91604

Adrian Zmed
23500 Daisy Trail
Calabasas, CA 91302

Music

They're Not A Star Until
They're A Star In Star Guide™

A _____ A

ABBA
Box 26072, S-100 41
Stockholm, SWEDEN

Paula Abdul
14820 McCormick
Van Nuys, CA 91411

Roy Acuff
2804 Opryland Drive
Nashville, TN 37214

Bryan Adams
406 - 68 Water Street
Vancouver, BC, V6B 1A3 CANADA

ADC Band
17397 Santa Barbara
Detroit, MI 48221

Janes's Addiction
8800 Sunset Blvd. #401
Los Angeles, CA 90069

A-HA
P.O. Box 203
Watford, WD1 3YA, ENGLAND

Air Supply
1990 S. Bundy Drive #590
Los Angeles, CA 90025

Alabama
P.O. Box 529
Ft. Payne, AL 35967

Peter Allen
6 W. 77th Street
New York, NY 10022

Mose Allison
34 Dogwood Street
Smithtown, NY 11787

Greg Allman
P.O. Box 4332
Marietta, GA 30061

Herb Alpert
31930 Pacific Coast Hwy.
Malibu, CA 90265

America
8730 Sunset Blvd. #PH
Los Angeles, CA 90069

Lynn Anderson
4025 Tyne Valley Blvd.
Nashville, TN 37220

Marian Anderson
Marianna Farms
Joe's Hill Road
Danbury, CT 06811

Julie Andrews
P.O. Box 666
Beverly Hills, CA 90213

Paul Anka
P.O. Box 100
Carmel, CA 93921

Adam Ant
170 Kings Road
London, SW3, ENGLAND

Apollonia
9000 Sunset Blvd. #1112
Los Angeles, CA 90069

Joan Armatrading
27 Queensdale Place
London, W11, ENGLAND

Ashford & Simpson
254 W. 72nd Street #1A
New York, NY 10023

Vladimir Ashkenazv
Sonnenhof 4
6004, Lucerne, SWITZERLAND

Rick Astley
4 - 7 The Vineyard Sanctuary
London, SE1 1QL, ENGLAND

Chet Atkins
1012 - 17th Avenue South
Nashville, TN 37212

Frankie Avalon
1652 Aldercreek Place
Westlake Village, CA 91362

Hoyt Axton
3135 Cedarwood
Tahoe City, CA 95730

Charles Aznavour
4 Avenue De Lieulee
78, Galluis, FRANCE

B   B

B-52's
Box 506, Canal Street Station
New York, NY 10013

Babyface
P.O. Box 921729
Atlanta, GA 30092

Burt Bacharach
658 Nimes Road
Los Angeles, CA 90077

Joan Baez
P.O. Box 1026
Menlo Park, CA 94025

Anita Baker
804 N. Crescent Drive
Beverly Hills, CA 90210

Shirley Bassey (c/o Novak)
Villa Capricorn
55 Via Campione
6816, Bissone, SWITZERLAND

Bay City Rollers
27 Preston Grange Road
Preston Pans.
E. Lothian, SCOTLAND

Beach Boys
101 Mesa Lane
Santa Barbara, CA 93109

Beastie Boys
298 Elizabeth Street
New York, NY 10012

Beatlemania
P.O. Box 262
Carteret, NY 17008

Jeff Beck
11 Old S. Lincolns Inn
London, WC2, ENGLAND

Bee-Gees
1755 - 149th Street N.E.
Miami Beach, FL 33181

Harry Belafonte
300 West End Avenue
New York, NY 10023

Bellamy Brothers
Rt. 2, Box 294
Dade City, FL 33525

Bell Biv Devoe
70 Universal City Plaza
Universal City, CA 91608

Pat Benatar
3575 Cahuenga Blvd. #470
Los Angeles, CA 90068

Tony Bennett
101 W. 55th Street #9A
New York, NY 10019

George Benson
19 Holomakani Place
La Haina, HI 96761

Berlin
1428 S. Sherbourne Drive
Los Angeles, CA 90035

Elmer Bernstein
1801 Avenue of the Stars #911
Los Angeles, CA 90067

Chuck Berry
Buckner Road - Berry Park
Wentzville, MO 63385

Clint Black
P.O. Box 19647
Houston, TX 77024

Blackfoot
17650 W. 12 Mile Road
Southfield, MI 48076

Bobby "Blue" Bland
3500 W. Olive Avenue #740
Burbank, CA 91505

Michael Bolton
201 W. 85th Street #15A
New York, NY 10024

Gary "US" Bonds
168 Orchid Drive
Pearl River, NY 10965

Bon Jovi
240 Central Park South
New York, NY 10019

Mayor Sonny Bono
1700 N. Indian Avenue
Palm Springs, CA 92262

Boomtown Rats
44 Seymour
London, W1, ENGLAND

Bobby Brown
18653 Ventura Blvd. #707
Tarzana, CA 91356

Debbie Boone
4334 Kester Avenue
Sherman Oaks, CA 91403

James Brown
810 - 7th Avenue
New York, NY 10019

Pat Boone
904 N. Beverly Drive
Beverly Hills, CA 90210

Les Brown
1455 Monaco Drive
Pacific Palisades, CA 90272

Victor Borge
Fieldpoint Park
Greenwich, CT 06830

T. Graham Brown
1516 - 16th Avenue South
Nashville, TN 37212

David Bowie
641 - 5th Avenue #22Q
New York, NY 10022

Jackson Browne
3208 Cahuenga Blvd. West #108
Los Angeles, CA 90068

Boxcar Willie
1300 Division Street #103
Nashville, TN 37203

Dave Brubeck
221 Millstone Road
Wilton, CT 06897

The Boys
6255 Sunset Blvd. #1700
Los Angeles, CA 90028

Lindsey Buckingham
900 Airole Way
Los Angeles, CA 90077

Boys Don't Cry
3 Wansdown Pl., Fulham, Broadway
London, SW6 1DN, ENGLAND

Jimmy Buffett
500 Duval Street #B
Key West, FL 33040

Brand X
17171 Roscoe Blvd. #104
Northridge, CA 91325

T-Bone Burnett
211 - 20th Street
Santa Monica, CA 90402

Garth Brooks
1109 - 17th Avenue South
Nashville, TN 37212

Charlie Byrd
3223 "K" Street NW
Washington, DC 20007

C   C

Shirley Caesar
10100 Santa Monica Blvd. #1600
Los Angeles, CA 90067

Sammy Cahn
704 N. Canon Drive
Beverly Hills, CA 90210

Cab Calloway
1040 Knollwood Road
White Plains, NY 10603

Glen Campbell
5290 Exeter Blvd.
Phoenix, AZ 85018

Freddie Cannon
18641 Cassandra Street
Beverly Hills, CA 91356

The Captain & Tennille
P.O. Box 262
Glenbrook, NV 89413

Irene Cara
8033 Sunset Blvd. #735
Los Angeles, CA 90046

Mariah Carey
c/o CBS Records
51 W. 52nd Street
New York, NY 10019

Belinda Carlisle
3907 W. Alameda Avenue #200
Burbank, CA 91505

Kim Carnes
737 Latimer Road
Santa Monica, CA 90402

Richard Carpenter
8341 Lubec Avenue
Downey, CA 90240

Vikki Carr
2289 Betty Lane
Beverly Hills, CA 90210

Jose Carreras
via Augusta 59
E-08006 Barcelona SPAIN

Johnny Cash
711 Summerfield Drive
Hendersonville, TN 37075

David Cassidy
701 N. Oakhurst Drive
Beverly Hills, CA 90210

Shaun Cassidy
8899 Beverly Blvd.
Los Angeles, CA 90048

Tracy Chapman
506 Santa Monica Blvd. #400
Santa Monica, CA 90401

Ray Charles
4863 Southridge Avenue
Los Angeles, CA 90008

Cheap Trick
315 W. Gorham Street
Madison, WI 53703

Natalie Cole
4201 3/4 Cahuenga Blvd.
North Hollywood, CA 91602

Chubby Checker
1650 Broadway #1011
New York, NY 10019

Judy Collins
845 West End Avenue
New York, NY 10024

Chicago
345 N. Maple Drive #235
Beverly Hills, CA 90210

Phil Collins
Lockswood
Sussex, ENGLAND

Toni Childs
888 - 7th Avenue #1602
New York, NY 10019

Jessie Colter
1117 - 17th Avenue South
Nashville, TN 37212

Eric Clapton
67 Brook Street
London, W1, ENGLAND

The Commodores
3151 Cahuenga Blvd. W. #235
Los Angeles, CA 90068

Dick Clark
3003 W. Olive Avenue
Burbank, CA 91505

Perry Como
305 Northern Blvd. #3A
Great Neck, NY 11021

Petula Clark
410 Park Avenue, 10th Floor
New York, NY 10022

Rita Coolidge
1330 N. Wetherly Drive
Los Angeles, CA 90069

Roy Clark
1800 Forrest Blvd.
Tulsa, OK 74114

Alice Cooper
4135 E. Keim Street
Paradise Valley, AZ 85253

Van Cliburn
455 Wilder Place
Shreveport, LA 71104

Stewart Copeland
9313 Doheny Road
Beverly Hills, CA 90210

The Coasters
9227 Nichols Street
Bellflower, CA 90706

Chick Corea
2635 Griffith Park Blvd.
Los Angeles, CA 90039

Elvis Costello
9028 Great West Road
Middlesex TW8 9EW, ENGLAND

Billy "Crash" Craddock
1020 E. Wendover Ave. #202
Greensboro, NC 27405

The Crickets
Rt. 1, Box 222
Lyles, TN 37098

Peter Criss
645 Madison Avenue
New York, NY 10022

Bob Crosby
939 Coast Blvd.
La Jolla, CA 92037

David Crosby
17351 Rancho Street
Encino, CA 91316

Christopher Cross
P.O. Box 23021
Santa Barbara, CA 93103

Andre Crouch
1821 Wilshire Blvd #200
Santa Monica, CA 90403

Rodney Crowell
1114 - 17th Avenue South #101
Nashville, TN 37212

Culture Club
34A Green Lane
Northwood, Middlesex, ENGLAND

D_____D

Roger Daltry
48 Harley House
Marlebone Road
London, NW1 5HL, ENGLAND

Vic Damone
P.O. Box 2999
Beverly Hills, CA 90213

Charlie Daniels Band
Rt. 6, Box 156A
Lebanon, TX 37087

Terence Trent D'Arby
Churchworks N. Villas
London, NW1 9AY ENGLAND

Miles Davis
315 W. 70th Street
New York, NY 10023

Taylor Dayne
2288 Jerusalem Avenue
North Bellmore, NY 11710

Jimmy Dean
24 Music Square West
Nashville, TN 37203

De Barge
205 Hill Street
Santa Monica, CA 90405

Deep Purple
P.O. Box 254
Sheffield, S6 1DF, ENGLAND

Rick Dees
8 Toluca Estates Drive
Toluca Lake, CA 91602

Def Leppard
80 Warwick Gardens
London, W14 8PR, ENGLAND

Penny DeHaven
P.O. Box 83
Brentwood, TN 37027

John Denver
P.O. Box 1587
Aspen, CO 81612

Depeche Mode
429 Harrow Road
London, W10 4RE, ENGLAND

Neil Diamond
161 S. Mapleton Drive
Los Angeles, CA 90077

Dire Straits
#10 Southwick Mews
London, W2, ENGLAND

D.J. Jazzy Jeff &
The Fresh Prince
298 Elizabeth Street
New York, NY 10012

Mickey Dolenz
2921 W. Alameda Avenue
Burbank, CA 91505

Placido Domingo
10601 Wilshire Blvd. #1502
Los Angeles, CA 90024

Fats Domino
5515 Marais Street
New Orleans, LA 70117

Doobie Brothers
15140 Sonoma Hwy.
Glen Ellen, CA 95442

The Doors
2548 Hutton Drive
Beverly Hills, CA 90210

The Drifters
10 Chelsea Court
Neptune, NJ 07753

Peter Duchin
305 Madison Avenue #956
New York, NY 10165

Sandy Duncan
10390 Santa Monica Blvd. #300
Los Angeles, CA 90025

Holly Dunn
P.O. Box 128037
Nashville, TN 37212

Duran Duran
P.O. Box 600
London, NW18 1EN, ENGLAND

Bob Dylan
P.O. Box 264, Cooper Station
New York, NY 10003

E   E

Earth, Wind & Fire
11340 W. Olympic Blvd. #357
Los Angeles, CA 90064

Sheena Easton
3575 Cahuenga Blvd. W. #470
Los Angeles, CA 90068

Billy Eckstine
1118 - 15th Street #4
Santa Monica, CA 90403

Larry Elgart
55 E. 74th Street
New York, NY 10021

Gloria Estefan
8390 S.W. 4th Street
Miami, FL 33144

Melissa Etheridge
3800 Barham Blvd. #309
Los Angeles, CA 90068

Europe
Box 22036, S-104 - 22
Stockholm, SWEDEN

Eurythmics
Box 245
London, N89 QG, ENGLAND

Everly Brothers
P.O. Box 2605
Nashville, TN 37219

Exile
P.O. Box 23341
Lexington, KY 40523

F   F

Marianne Faithfull
Yew Tree Cottage
Aldworth, Berks., ENGLAND

Lola Falana
P.O. Box 50369
Henderson, NV 89016

Fat Boys
250 W. 57th Street #1723
New York, NY 10107

Dr. Feelgood
3 E. 54th Street
New York, NY 10022

Jose Feliciano
266 Lyons Plain Road
Weston, CT 06883

Freddy Fender
5626 Brock Street
Houston, TX 77023

Maynard Ferguson
P.O. Box 716
Ojai, CA 93023

Fine Young Cannibals
1680 N. Vine Street #1101
Los Angeles, CA 90028

The Firm
57A Great Titchfield Street
London, W1P 7FL, ENGLAND

Ella Fitzgerald
908 N. Whittier Drive
Beverly Hills, CA 90210

Roberta Flack
1 West 72nd Street
New York, NY 10023

Fleetwood Mac
39169 W. Heathercliff #574
Malibu, CA 90265

Mick Fleetwood
11435 Bellagio Road
Los Angeles, CA 90049

Myron Floren
26 Georgeff Road
Rolling Hills, CA 90274

Dan Fogelberg
Mountain Bird Ranch
Box 824
Pagosa Springs, CO 81147

"Tennessee" Ernie Ford
255 Mathache Drive
Portola Valley, CA 94025

Foreigner
1790 Broadway, PH
New York, NY 10019

Forester Sisters
128 Volunteer Drive
Hendersonville, TN 37075

The Four Seasons
P.O. Box 262
Carteret, NJ 07008

Samantha Fox
11 Mt. Pleasant Villa
London, 4HH, ENGLAND

Peter Frampton
2669 Larmar Road
Los Angeles, CA 90068

Connie Francis
7305 W. Sample Road #101
Coral Springs, FL 33065

Frankie Goes to Hollywood
153 George Street
London, W1, ENGLAND

Aretha Franklin
P.O. Box 12137
Birmingham, MI 48012

Fresh
306 S. Salina Street #316
Syracuse, NY 13202

Janie Fricke
P.O. Box 680785
San Antonio, TX 78268

G   G

Kenny G
21940 Lamplighter
Malibu, CA 90265

Peter Gabriel
13 Abbie Church Yard
Bath, ENGLAND

Art Garfunkel
9 E. 79th Street
New York, NY 10021

Larry Gatlin
7003 Chadwick Drive #360
Brentwood, TN 37027

Crystal Gayle
51 Music Square East
Nashville, TN 37203

David Geffen
9130 Sunset Blvd.
Los Angeles, CA 90069

Sir Bob Geldof
Davington Priory
London, ENGLAND

Genesis
81 - 83 Walton Street
London, NW3, ENGLAND

Boy George (O'Dowd)
34A Green Lane
Northwood, Middlesex
ENGLAND

Barry Gibb
3088 South Mann
Las Vegas, NV 89102

Debbie Gibson
P.O. Box 489
Merrick, NY 11566

Johnny Gill
9229 Sunset Blvd. #311
Los Angeles, CA 90069

Vince Gill
1514 South Street
Nashville, TN 37212

Dizzy Gillespie
477 N. Woodlands
Englewood, NJ 07632

Mickey Gilley
P.O. Box 1242
Pasadena, TX 77501

Philip Glass
231 - 2nd Avenue
New York, NY 10003

Bobby Goldsboro
P.O. Box 5250
Ocala, FL 32678

Berry Gordy
878 Stradella Road
Los Angeles, CA 90077

Lesley Gore
170 E. 77th Street #2A
New York, NY 10021

Grateful Dead
Box 1566, Main Station
Montclair, NJ 07043

Eydie Gorme
820 Greenway Drive
Beverly Hills, CA 90210

Lee Greenwood
1311 Elm Hill Pike
Nashville, TN 37214

Robert Goulet
3110 Monte Rosa
Las Vegas, NV 89120

Guns & Roses
1830 S. Robertson Blvd. #201
Los Angeles, CA 90035

Amy Grant
120 - 30th Avenue North
Nashville, TN 37203

Arlo Guthrie
250 W. 57th Street #1304
New York, NY 10019

H   H

Merle Haggard
P.O. Box 536
Palo Cedro, CA 96073

Lionel Hampton
20 W. 64th Styreet #28K
New York, NY 10023

Hall & Oates
130 W. 57th Street #2A
New York, NY 10019

Herbie Hancock
1250 N. Doheny Drive
Los Angeles, CA 90069

Tom T. Hall
P.O. Box 37065
Franklin, TN 37065

EmmyLou Harris
P.O. Box 1384
Brentwood, TN 37027

Marvin Hamlisch
970 Park Avenue #65
New York, NY 10028

George Harrison
Friar Park Road
Henly-On-Thames, ENGLAND

M.C. Hammer
80 Swan Way #130
Oakland, CA 94621

Deborah Harry
425 W. 21st Street
New York, NY 10011

Corey Hart
81 Hymus Blvd.
Montreal, PQ Que. H9R 1E2
CANADA

Isaac Hayes
1962 Spectrum Circle #700
Marietta, GA 30067

Florence Henderson
P.O. Box 11295
Marina del Rey, CA 90295

Don Henley
14100 Mulholland Drive
Beverly Hills, CA 90210

Highway 101
4155 E. Jewell #412
Denver, CO 80222

Al Hirt
809 St. Louis Street
New Orleans, LA 70112

Dr. Hook
P.O. Box 121017
Nashville, TN 37212

Linda Hopkins
2055 N. Ivar, PH
Los Angeles, CA 90069

Lena Horne
5950 Canoga Avenue #200
Woodland Hills, CA 91367

Bruce Hornsby
P.O. Box 3545
Williamsburg, VA 23187

Thelma Houston
4296 Mt. Vernon
Los Angeles, CA 90008

Whitney Houston
30 Northgate Road
Mendham Township, NJ 07945

Human League
P.O. Box 153
Sheffield, SL 1DR, ENGLAND

Englebert Humperdinck
10100 Sunset Blvd.
Los Angeles, CA 90077

Ferlin Huskey
38 Music Square E. #300
Nashville, CA 37203

Phyllis Hyman
P.O. Box 50
Philadelphia, PA 19103

I _____ I

Billy Idol
8209 Melrose Avenue
Los Angeles, CA 90046

Julio Inglesias
5 Indian Creek Drive
Miami, FL 33154

The Ink Spots
1385 York Avenue #15H
New York, NY 10021

INXS
145 Brougham Street, Kings Cross
Sydney, 2011 NSW, AUSTRALIA

Iron Maiden
P.O. Box 391
London, W4 1LZ, ENGLAND

The Isley Brothers
446 Liberty Road
Inglewood, NJ 07631

J   J

Janet Jackson
12546 The Vista
Los Angeles, CA 90049

Jermaine Jackson
4641 Hayvenhurst
Encino, CA 91316

Joe Jackson
6 Pembridge Road
Trinity House #200
London, W11, ENGLAND

LaToya Jackson
Waldorf Astoria
301 Park Avenue
New York, NY 10022

Marlon Jackson
4704 Balboa Blvd.
Encino, CA 91436

Michael Jackson
Sycamore Valley Ranch
Zacca Landeras
Santa Ynez, CA 93460

Rebbie Jackson
4641 Hayvenhurst Drive
Encino, CA 91316

Tito Jackson
15255 Del Gado Drive
Sherman Oaks, CA 91403

Mick Jagger
2 Munro Terrace
London, SW10 ODL, ENGLAND

Rick James
104 Chapin Parkway
Buffalo, NY 14209

Al Jarreau
16121 Morrison
Encino, CA 91316

Jay & The Americans
P.O. Box 262
Carteret, NJ 07008

Waylon Jennings
62 E. Starrs Plain Road
Danbury, CT 06810

Joan Jett
5700 - 39th Avenue
Hyattsville, MD 20781

The Jetts
Box 290097, Brooklyn Center
Minneapolis, MN 55429

Billy Joel
200 W. 57th Street #308
New York, NY 10019

Elton John
125 Kensington High Street
London, W1, ENGLAND

Johnny Hates Jazz
321 Fulham Road
London, SW10 9QL, ENGLAND

The Brothers Johnson
9200 Sunset Blvd. #823
Los Angeles, CA 90069

Davey Jones
21 Elms Road
Fareham, Hants., ENGLAND

Quincy Jones
P.O. Box 48249
Los Angeles, CA 90048

Rickie Lee Jones
888 - 7th Avenue #1602
New York, NY 10019

Tom Jones
363 Copa de Oro Road
Los Angeles, CA 90049

Journey
P.O. Box 404
San Francisco, CA 94101

Judas Priest
3 E. 54th Street #1400
New York, NY 10022

The Judds
P.O. Box 17087
Nashville, TN 37217

K   K

Casey Kasem
138 N. Mapleton Drive
Los Angeles, CA 90077

Eddie Kendricks
200 W. 57th Street #907
New York, NY 10019

B.B. King
P.O. Box 4396
Las Vegas, NV 89107

Carole King
P.O. Box 7308
Carmel, CA 93921

Evelyn "Champagne" King
119 W. 57th Street #901
New York, NY 10019

The Kingsmen
P.O. Box 2622
Asheville, NC 28801

The Kingston Trio
P.O. Box 34397
San Diego, CA 92103

John Knowles
P.O. Box 939
Southampton, NY 11968

Kiss
6363 Sunset Blvd. #417
Los Angeles, CA 90028

Kool & The Gang
614 Lexington Avenue
New York, NY 10022

Gladys Knight
98 Cuttermill Road
Box 82 - #342A
Great Neck, NY 11022

Lenny Kravitz
6435 Balcom
Reseda, CA 91335

Kris Kristofferson
3179 Sumack Ridge
Malibu, CA 90265

Holly Knight
1585 Stone Canyon Road
Los Angeles, CA 90077

L   L

Patti LaBelle
1212 Grennox Road
Wynnewood, PA 19096

Sean Lennon
1 W. 72nd Street
New York, NY 10023

K.D. Lang
1616 W. 3rd Avenue
Vancouver, BC V6J 1K2, CANADA

The Lennon Sisters
944 Harding Avenue
Venice, CA 90291

Cyndi Lauper
853 - 7th Avenue #9D
New York, NY 10019

Le Vert
110 - 112 Lantoga Road #D
Wayne, PA 19087

Brenda Lee
2126 N. North Street
Peoria, IL 61604

Huey Lewis
P.O. Box 819
Mill Valley, CA 94942

Julian Lennon
7319 Woodrow Wilson Drive
Los Angeles, CA 90046

Jerry Lee Lewis
P.O. Box 3864
Memphis, TN 38173

Gordon Lightfoot
1364 Yonge Street #207
Toronto, Ont. M4T 2P7 CANADA

Mark Lindsay
9595 Wilshire Blvd. #400
Beverly Hills, CA 90212

Lisa Lisa
747 - 10th Avenue
New York, NY 10019

Little River Band
87-91 Palmerstin Cres.
Albert Park
Melbourne Victoria 3206
AUSTRALIA

LL Cool J
298 Elizabeth Street
New York, NY 10012

Kenny Loggins
985 Hot Springs Road
Santa Barbara, CA 93108

Patty Loveless
P.O. Box 363
Groveport, OH 43125

Loverboy
406 - 68 Water Street
Gastown Vancouver,
BC VGB 1AY, CANADA

Lyle Lovett
1514 South Street
Nashville, TN 37212

Loretta Lynn
1010 - 18th Avenue South
Nashville, TN 37212

M_____M

Madonna
9200 Sunset Blvd. #915
Los Angeles, CA 90069

The Mamas & The Papas
805 Third Avenue #2900
New York, NY 10022

Melissa Manchester
15822 High Knoll Road
Encino, CA 91436

Henry Mancini
261 Baroda Drive
Los Angeles, CA 90077

Barbara Mandrell
128 River Road
Hendersonville, TN 37075

Erline Mandrell
713 W. Main Street
Hendersonville, TN 37075

Louise Mandrell
Old Hickory Lane
Hendersonville, TN 37075

Manhattan Transfer
3805 W. Magnolia Blvd.
Burbank, CA 91505

Barry Manilow
6640 Sunset Blvd. #200
Los Angeles, CA 90028

Teena Marie
1700 Broadway, 10th Floor
New York, NY 10019

Wynton Marsalis
4200 Argyle Tarrace N.W.
Washington, DC 20011

Johnny Mathis
3500 W. Olive Avenue #750
Burbank, CA 91505

Kathy Mattea
P.O. Box 158482
Nashville, TN 37215

Paul McCartney
Waterfall Estate Peamarsh
St. Leonard on the Sea
Sussex, ENGLAND

Marilyn McCoo
P.O. Box 7905
Beverly Hills, CA 90212

Reba McEntyre
511 Fairgrounds Court
Nashville, TN 37204

Bobby McFerrin
600 W. 58th Street #9188
New York, NY 10019

The McGuire Sisters
100 Rancho Circle
Las Vegas, NV 89119

Don McLean
Old Manitou Road
Garrison, NY 10524

Meatloaf
Box 68, Stockport
Cheshire, SK3 OJY, ENGLAND

John Cougar Mellencamp
Rt. 1, Box 361
Nashville, IN 47448

Harold Melvin
P.O. Box 82
Great Neck, NY 11021

Men at Work
Box 289
Abbotsford, Victoria, 3067
AUSTRALIA

Menudo
Padosa Hato Rey
157 Ponce de Leon
San Juan, PUERTO RICO

Yehudi Menuhin
165 W. 57th Street
New York, NY 10019

Freddy Mercury
5 Campden Street
London, W8, ENGLAND

Miami Sound Machine
8390 S.W. 4th Street
Miami, FL 33144

George Michael
2 Elgin Mews North
London, W9 1NN, ENGLAND

Bette Midler
P.O. Box 46703
Los Angeles, CA 90046

Mighty Clouds of Joy
9220 Sunset Blvd. #823
Los Angeles, CA 90069

Mike & The Mechanics
P.O. Box 107
London, N65 ARU ENGLAND

Mitch Miller
345 W. 58th Street
New York, NY 10019

Ronnie Milsap
12 Music Circle South
Nashville, TN 37203

Liza Minnelli
150 E. 69th Street #21G
New York, NY 10021

Missing Persons
11935 Laurel Hills Road
Studio City, CA 91604

Joni Mitchell
10960 Wilshire Blvd. #938
Los Angeles, CA 90024

The Monkees
Radio City Station, Box 1461
New York, NY 10101

Carlos Montoya
345 W. 58th Street
New York, NY 10019

Lorrie Morgan
818 - 18 Avenue South
Nashville, TN 37203

Gary Morris
6027 Church Drive
Sugarland, TX 77478

Van Morrison
12304 Santa Monica Blvd. #300
Los Angeles, CA 90025

Motley Crue
40/42 Newman Street
London, W1P 3PA, ENGLAND

Maria Muldaur
P.O. Box 5535
Mill Valley, CA 94942

Anne Murray
4881 Yonge Street #412
Toronto, Ontario, M4S 2B9,
CANADA

N_____N

Graham Nash
4800 Encino Avenue
Encino, CA 91316

Willie Nelson
P.O. Box 33280
Austin, TX 78764

Michael Nesmith
50 N. La Cienega Blvd. #210
Beverly Hills, CA 90211

Aaron Neville
10100 Santa Monica Blvd. #1600
Los Angeles, CA 90067

New Edition
P.O. Box 77505
San Francisco, CA 94107

New Kids on the Block
6 St. Gregory St., Box 7001
Dorchester, MA 02124

Tommy Newson
19315 Wells Drive
Tarzana, CA 91356

Wayne Newton
6629 S. Pecos
Las Vegas, NV 89120

Olivia Newton-John
P.O. Box 2710
Malibu, CA 90265

Stevie Nicks
P.O. Box 6907
Alhambra, CA 91802

Jessye Norman
c/o Shaw
1900 Broadway
New York, NY 10023

Ted Nugent
P.O. Box 15108
Ann Arbor, MI 48106

Gary Numan
39/41 North Road
London, N7 7DP, ENGLAND

Laura Nyro
P.O. Box 186
Shoreham, NY 11786

O _____ O

Oak Ridge Boys
329 Rockland Road
Hendersonville, TN 37075

Sinead O'Connor
10 Halsey House
13 Red Lyon Square
London, WC1, ENGLAND

O'Jays
113 N. Robertson Blvd.
Los Angeles, CA 90048

Mike Oldfield
"Little Halings"
Tilehouse Lane
Denham, Bucks, ENGLAND

Yoko Ono (Lennon)
One W. 72nd Street
New York, NY 10023

Tony Orlando
151 El Camino Drive
Beverly Hills, CA 90212

Jeffery Osbourne
5800 Valley Oak Drive
Los Angeles, CA 90068

Ozzy Osbourne
184 Sutherland Ave., Flat #2
London, W9, ENGLAND

K. T. Oslin
1103 - 16th Avenue
Nashville, TN 37212

Donny Osmond
1570 Brookhollow Drive #118
Santa Ana, CA 92714

Marie Osmond
3325 N. University #375
Provo, UT 84605

Paul Overstreet
P.O. Box 2977
Hendersonville, TN 37077

P _____ P

Pablo Cruise
P.O. Box 779
Mill Valley, CA 94941

Patti Page
1413 San Lucas Court
Solana Beach, CA 92075

Robert Palmer
2A Chelsea Manor
Blood Street
London, SW3, ENGLAND

Johnny Paris
1764 Parkway Drive South
Maumee, OH 43537

Alan Parsons Project
30 The Avenue Muswell Hill
London, N10, ENGLAND

Dolly Parton
Crockett Road, Rt #1
Brentwood, TN 37027

Randy Parton
821 - 19th Avenue South
Nashville, TN 37202

Les Paul
78 Deerhaven Road
Mahwah, NJ 07430

Luciano Pavarotti
941 Via Giardini
41040 Saliceta S. Guiliano
Modena, ITALY

Johnny Paycheck #208-791
Madison Correctional Institute
P.O. Box 740
London, OH 43140

Freda Payne
10160 Cielo Drive
Beverly Hills, CA 90210

Minnie Pearl
874 Curtiswood Lane
Nashville, TN 37204

Pebble
8730 Sunset Blvd. #PH West
Los Angeles, CA 90069

Teddy Pendergrass
1505 Flat Rock Road
Narberth, PA 19072

The Penguins
708 W. 137th Street
Gardena, CA 90247

Carl Perkins
459 Country Club Lane
Jackson, TN 38301

Itzhak Perlman
173 Riverside Drive #3C
New York, NY 10024

Peter, Paul & Mary
853 - 7th Avenue
New York, NY 10019

Pet Shop Boys
101 - 109 Ladbroke Grove
London, W11, ENGLAND

Tom Petty
500 S. Sepulveda Blvd. #500
Los Angeles, CA 90049

Michelle Phillips
3930 Legion Lane
Los Angeles, CA 90039

Wilson Pickett
200 W. 57th Street #907
New York, NY 10019

Ray Pillow
2401 - 12th Avenue South
Nashville, TN 37204

Pink Floyd
43 Portland Road
London, W11, ENGLAND

The Platters
P.O. Box 39
Las Vegas, NV 89101

The Pointer Sisters
10100 Santa Monica Blvd. #1600
Los Angeles, CA 90067

The Police
194 Kensington Park Road
London, W11 2ES, ENGLAND

Iggy Pop
449 S. Beverly Drive #101
Beverly Hills, CA 90212

Andre Previn
8 Sherwood Lane
Bedford Hills, NY 10507

Leontyne Price
9 Van Dam Street
New York, NY 10003

Charlie Pride
3198 Royal Lane #204
Dallas, TX 75229

Prince
9401 Kiowa Trail
Chanhassen, MN 55317

Q_____Q

Quarterflash
P.O. Box 8231
Portland, OR 97207

Queen
46 Pembridge Road
London, W11 3HN, ENGLAND

R_____R

Eddie Rabbitt
4808 La Villa Marina #F
Marina del Rey, CA 90291

Gerry Rafferty
51 Paddington Street
London, W1, ENGLAND

Bonnie Raitt
P.O. Box 626
Los Angeles, CA 90078

Ratt
1818 Illion Street
San Diego, CA 92110

Eddy Raven
P.O. Box 1402
Hendersonville, TN 37075

Lou Rawls
109 Fremont Place
Los Angeles, CA 90005

Helen Reddy
2645 Outpost Road
Los Angeles, CA 90068

Jerry Reed
116 Wilson Park #210
Brentwood, TN 37027

Martha Reeves
168 Orchid Drive
Pearl River, NY 10965

Paul Revere & The Raiders
9000 Sunset Blvd. #315
Los Angeles, CA 90069

James Reynolds
1925 Hamscom Drive
South Pasadena, CA 91030

Cliff Richard
St. Greorge's Hill
Weybridge, ENGLAND

Little Richard
Hyatt Sunset Hotel
8401 Sunset Blvd
Los Angeles, CA 90069

Keith Richards
"Redlands",
West Wittering
Chichester, Sussex, ENGLAND

Lionel Richie
5750 Wilshire Blvd. #590
Los Angeles, CA 90036

Righteous Brothers
9841 Hot Springs Drive
Huntington Beach, CA 92646

Jeannie C. Riley
P.O. Box 454
Brentwood, TN 37027

The Ritchie Family
4100 W. Flagler #B-2
Miami, FL 33134

Smokey Robinson
17085 Rancho Street
Encino, CA 91316

Johnny Rodriquez
P.O. Box 2671
Nashville, TN 37219

Kenny Rogers
Rt. 1, Box 100
Colbert, GA 30628

Rolling Stones
1776 Broadway #4419
New York, NY 10165

Linda Ronstadt
5750 Wilshire Blvd. #590
Los Angeles, CA 90036

Diana Ross
Box 11059, Glenville Station
Greenwich, CT 06831

David Lee Roth
3960 Laurel Canyon Blvd. #430
Studio City, CA 91604

Billy Joe Royal
819 - 18th Street South
Nashville, TN 37203

Rufus
7250 Beverly Blvd. #200
Los Angeles, CA 90036

Run-D.M.C.
296 Elizabeth Street
New York, NY 10012

Brenda Russell
9000 Sunset Blvd. #1200
Los Angeles, CA 90069

Bobby Rydell
917 Bryn Mawr Avenue
Narberth, PA 19072

S   S

Sade
Morgans Hotel
237 Madison Avenue
New York, NY 10016

Carole Bayer Sager
658 Nimes Road
Los Angeles, CA 90077

Buffy Sainte-Marie
RR #1, Box 368
Kapaa, Kauai, HI 96746

Santana
P.O. Box 26671
San Francisco, CA 94126

Boz Scaggs
345 N. Maple Drive #235
Beverly Hills, CA 90210

Lalo Schifrin
710 N. Hillcrest Road
Beverly Hills, CA 90210

Scorpions
Box 5220
3000, Hanover, GERMANY

Earl Scruggs
P.O. Box 66
Madison, TN 37115

John Sebastian
12744 Weddington
North Hollywood, CA 91607

Neil Sedaka
8787 Shoreham Drive
Los Angeles, CA 90069

Pete Seeger
Duchess Junction, Box 431
Beacon, NY 12508

The Serenpidity Singers
P.O. Box 399
Lisle, IL 60532

Doc Severinsen
2807 Nichols Canyon
Los Angeles, CA 90046

Paul Shaffer
30 Rockefeller Plaza #1410W
New York, NY 10020

Sam the Sham
3667 Tetwiler Avenue
Memphis, TN 38122

Artie Shaw
2127 W. Palos Court
Newbury Park, CA 91320

Tommy Shaw
1790 Broadway PH
New York, NY 10019

Sheila E
9830 Wilshire Blvd.
Beverly Hills, CA 90212

Dinah Shore
916 Oxford Way
Beverly Hills, CA 90210

Beverly Sills
211 Central Park West
New York, NY 10024

Gene Simmons
6363 Sunset Blvd. #417
Los Angeles, CA 90028

Carly Simon
135 Central Park West
New York, NY 10023

Paul Simon
1619 Broadway #500
New York, NY 10019

Nina Simone
1995 Broadway #501
New York, NY 10023

Simply Red
36 Atwood Road
Didsbury, Manchester 20
ENGLAND

Frank Sinatra
70 - 588 Frank Sinatra Drive
Rancho Mirage, CA 92270

Frank Sinatra, Jr.
2211 Florian Place
Beverly Hills, CA 90210

Nancy Sinatra
P.O. Box 69453
Los Angeles, CA 90069

Ricky Skaggs
P.O. Box 15781
Nashville, TN 37215

Skid Row
9229 Sunset Blvd. #710
Los Angeles, CA 90069

Grace Slick
18 Escalon Drive
Mill Valley, CA 94941

Hank Snow
P.O. Box 1084
Nashville, TN 37202

Sir Georg Solti
Chalet Haut Pre
1884 Villars-sur Ollon
SWITZERLAND

Phil Spector
1210 S. Arroyo Blvd.
Pasadena, CA 91101

Ronnie Spector
7 Maplecrest Drive
Danbury, CT 06810

Spinners
65 W. 55th Street #6C
New York, NY 10019

Split Ends
136 New Kings Road
London, SW6, ENGLAND

Rick Springfield
3510 Cross Creek Lane
Malibu, CA 90265

Bruce Springsteen
9922 Tower Lane
Beverly Hills, CA 90210

Billy Squier
71 Baker Street
London, W1M 1AH, ENGLAND

Lisa Stansfield
43 Hillcrest Road
Rockdale, ENGLAND

Ringo Starr
Tittenhurst Park
Ascot, Surrey, ENGLAND

Starship
1319 Bridgeway
Sausalito, CA 94965

Statler Brothers
P.O. Box 2703
Staunton, VA 24401

Tommy Steele
37 Hill Street
London, W1X 8JY, ENGLAND

Isaac Stern
211 Central Park West
New York, NY 10024

Cat Stevens (Yusef Islam)
Ariola Steinhauser Str. 3
8000, Munich, 80, GERMANY

Connie Stevens
9551 Cherokee Lane
Beverly Hills, CA 90210

Shadoe Stevens
10430 Wilshire Blvd. #2006
Los Angeles, CA 90024

Rod Stewart
391 N. Carolwood
Los Angeles, CA 90077

Stephen Stills
1636 Summitridge Drive
Beverly Hills, CA 90210

Sting
2 The Grove,
Highgate Village
London, N16, ENGLAND

Sly Stone
6255 Sunset Blvd. #200
Los Angeles, CA 90028

Stray Cats
113 Wardour Street
London, W1, ENGLAND

Barbra Streisand
301 N. Carolwood Drive
Los Angeles, CA 90077

Woody Strode
P.O. Box 501
Glendora, CA 91740

Marty Stuart
38 Music Square #218
Nashville, TN 37203

Donna Summer
714 W. Potrero Road
Thousand Oaks, CA 91361

Al B. Sure!
636 Warren Street
Brooklyn, NY 11217

Survivor
2114 W. Pico Blvd.
Santa Monica, CA 90405

Joan Sutherland
c/o Colbert Artists
111 W. 57th Street
New York, NY 10019

The Sylvers
1900 Avenue of the Stars #1600
Los Angeles, CA 90067

T   T

Taco
8124 W. 3rd Street #204
Los Angeles, CA 90048

Talking Heads
1775 Broadway #700
New York, NY 10019

Bernie Taupin
1320 N. Doheny Drive
Los Angeles, CA 90069

James Taylor
644 N. Doheny Drive
Los Angeles, CA 90069

Tears For Fears
50 New Bond Street
London, W1, ENGLAND

B.J. Thomas
P.O. Box 120003
Arlington, TX 76012

Michael Tilson Thomas
24 W. 57th Street
New York, NY 10019

The Thompson Twins
9 Eccleston Street
London, SW1, ENGLAND

Three Degrees
19 The Willows
Maidenhead Road
Windsor, Berk, ENGLAND

Three Dog Night
151 S. El Camino Drive
Beverly Hills, CA 90212

Tiffany
11337 Burbank Blvd.
N. Hollywood, CA 91601

Mel Tillis
908 - 18th Ave. South
Nashville, TN 37203

Tiny Tim
Hotel Olcott
27 W. 72nd Street
New York, NY 10023

Mel Torme
1734 Coldwater Canyon
Beverly Hills, CA 90210

Liz Torres
1711 North Avenue #53
Los Angeles, CA 90042

Toto
P.O. Box 7308
Carmel, CA 93921

Pete Townshend
48 Harley House
Marlebone Road
London, NW1, ENGLAND

Randy Travis
P.O. Box 121712
Nashville, TN 37212

Joey Travolta
4975 Chimineas Avenue
Tarzana, CA 91356

Travis Tritt
1112 N. Sherbourne Drive
Los Angeles, CA 90069

Marshall Tucker Band
300 E. Henry Street
Spartanburg, SC 69302

Tanya Tucker
2325 Crestmoor Rd.,Box 15245
Nashville, TN 37215

Jethro Tull
12 Stratford Place
London, W1N 9AF, ENGLAND

Tina Turner
Lindenallee 86
D-5000 Koln 51, GERMANY

Conway Twitty
#1 Music Village Blvd.
Hendersonville, TN 37075

2 Live Crew
8400 N.E. 2nd Avenue
Miami, FL 33138

U   U

U2
4 Windmill Lane
Dublin, 2, IRELAND

U.F.O.
10 Sutherland
London, W9 24Q, ENGLAND

Uriah Heep
150 Southhampton Row
London, WC1, ENGLAND

Utopia
132 Nassau Street
New York, NY 10038

V   V

June Valli
1158 Briar Way
Ft. Lee, NJ 07024

Richard Van Allen
18 Octavia Street
London, SW11 3DN, ENGLAND

Luther Vandross
1414 Seabright Drive
Beverly Hills, CA 90210

Vangelis
195 Queens Gate
London, W1, ENGLAND

Eddie Van Halen
10100 Santa Monica Blvd. #2460
Los Angeles, CA 90067

The Vapors
44 Balmoral Drive
Woking, Surrey, ENGLAND

Vanilla Ice
1290 Avenue of the Americas #4200
New York, NY 10104

Bobby Vee
P.O. Box 41
Sauk Rapids, MN 56379

Vanity
151 S. El Camino Drive
Beverly Hills, CA 90212

The Ventures
P.O. Box 1646
Burbank, CA 91507

Ricky Van Sheldon
Rt. 12, Box 95
Lebanon, TN 37087

Bobby Vinton
1905 Cold Canyon Road
Calabasas, CA 91302

W   W

Porter Wagoner
1830 Airlane Drive
Nashville, TN 37210

Kitty Wells
240 Old Hickory Blvd.
Madison, TN 35115

Junior Walker
141 Dunbar Avenue
Fords, NJ 08863

Dottie West
P.O. Box 2977
Madison, TN 37115

Dionne Warwick
806 N. Elm Drive
Beverly Hills, CA 90210

Barry White
10502 Whipple
North Hollywood, CA 91602

Jody Watley
8439 Sunset Blvd. #103
Los Angeles, CA 90069

White Snake
15 Poulton Road,Wallasey
Cheshire, ENGLAND

Lawrence Welk
1221 Ocean Avenue #602
Santa Monica, CA 90401

Slim Whitman
1300 Division Street #103
Nashville, TN 37203

Roger Whittaker
50 Regents Park Road
Primrose Hill
London, NW1, ENGLAND

The Who
48 Harley House
Marlebone Road
London, NW1, ENGLAND

Wild Cherry
28001 Chagrin Blvd. #205
Cleveland, OH 44122

Andy Williams
816 N. La Cienega Blvd.
Los Angeles, CA 90069

Deniece Williams
1414 Seabright
Beverly Hills, CA 90210

Don Williams
1103 - 16th Avenue South
Nashville, TN 37203

Hank Williams, Jr.
P.O. Box 850
Paris, TN 38242

Joe Williams
3337 Knollwood Court
Las Vegas, NV 89121

John Williams
301 Massachusetts Avenue
Boston, MA 02115

Paul Williams
645 Sand Point Road
Carpinteria, CA 93013

Vanessa Williams
Rt. #100
Millwood, NY 10546

Carl Dean Wilson
8860 Even View Drive
Los Angeles, CA 90069

Mary Wilson
5406 Red Oak Drive
Los Angeles, CA 90068

Nancy Wilson
5455 Wilshire Blvd. #1606
Los Angeles, CA 90036

Wilson Phillips
1290 Avenue of the Americas #4200
New York, NY 10104

Steve Winwood
888 - 7th Avenue #1602
New York, NY 10106

Wolfman Jack
P.O. Box 38
Belvidere, NC 27919

Bobby Womack
10713 Third Avenue
Inglewood, CA 90303

Stevie Wonder
2451 Chiselhurst Drive
Los Angeles, CA 90027

Tammy Wynette
P.O. Box 7532
Richboro, PA 18059

Y　　　　　　　　　　　　　　　　　　Y

"Weird" Al Yankovic
8842 Hollywood Blvd.
Los Angeles, CA 90069

Yanni
8002 Wilson Glen
Los Angeles, CA 90046

Yellowjackets
9220 Sunset Blvd. #320
Los Angeles, CA 90069

Dwight Yoakum
15840 Ventura Blvd. #465
Encino, CA 91436

Neil Young
3025 Surry Street
Los Angeles, CA 90027

Young M.C.
9229 Sunset Blvd. #319
Los Angeles, CA 90069

Z　　　　　　　　　　　　　　　　　　Z

Dweezil Zappa
7885 Woodrow Wilson Drive
Los Angeles, CA 90046

Frank Zappa
7885 Woodrow Wilson Drive
Los Angeles, CA 90046

Moon Zappa
10377 Oletha Lane
Los Angeles, CA 90077

ZZ Top
P.O. Box 19744
Houston, TX 77024

Sports

A   A

Henry "Hank" Aaron
1611 Adams Drive S.W.
Atlanta, GA 30311

Kareem Abdul-Jabbar
1170 Stone Canyon Road
Los Angeles, CA 90077

Akeem Abdul-Olajuwon
10 Greenway Plaza East
Houston, TX 77046

Rick Adelman
700 N.E. Multnomah Street. #600
Portland, OR 97232

Andre Agassi
6739 Tara Avenue
Las Vegas, NV 89102

Mark Aguirre
The Palace
Auburn Hills, MI 48057

Troy Aikman
1 Cowboys Parkway
Irving, TX 78063

Marv Albert
c/o NBC Sports
30 Rockefeller Plaza
New York, NY 10020

Muhammad Ali
P.O. Box 187
Berrien Springs, MI 49103

Marcus Allen
11745 Montana Avenue
Los Angeles, CA 90049

Bobby Allison
140 Church Street
Hueytown, AL 35020

George "Sparky" Anderson
Tiger Stadium
Detroit, MI 48216

Andre The Giant
P.O. Box 3859
Stamford, CT 06905

Mario Andretti
53 Victory Lane
Nazareth, PA 18064

Michael Andretti
505 East Eulia Avenue
Compton, CA 90224

Arthur Ashe
370 E. 76th Street #A-1402
New York, NY 10021

Red Auerbach
4200 Massachusetts Ave. N.W.
Washington, DC 20016

Tracy Austin
3601 W. Hidden Lane #304
Palos Verdes Estates, CA 90274

B
B

Tai Babilonia
1925 Century Park East #800
Los Angeles, CA 90067

Harold Baines
Oakland-Alameda Coliseum
Oakland, CA 94621

Seve Ballesteros
Pedrena
Santander, SPAIN

Ernie Banks
P.O. Box 24302
Los Angeles, CA 90024

Sir Roger Bannister
16 Edwards Square
London, W8, ENGLAND

Red Barber
3013 Brookmont Drive
Tallahassee, FL 32312

Jesse Barfield
River Avenue & E. 16th Street
Bronx, NY 10451

Charles Barkley
P.O. Box 25040
Philiadelphia, PA 19147

Carling Bassett
2665 S. Bay Shore #1002
Miami, FL 33133

Andy Bean
P.O. Box 12458
Palm Beach Gardens, FL 33410

Boris Becker
Nusslocher Strasst 51
6906, Leiman, GERMANY

George Bell
324 W. 35th Street
Chicago, IL 60616

Johnny Bench
661 Reisling Knoll
Cincinnati, OH 45226

Yogi Berra
19 Highland Avenue
Montclair, NJ 07042

Gary Bettenhausen
2550 Tree Farm Road
Martinsville, IN 46151

Tony Bettenhausen
5234 Wilton Wood Court
Indianapolis, IN 46254

Craig Biggio
Astrodome
Houston, TX 77001

Matt Biondi
1025 Thomas Jefferson Street N.W.
Suite #450E
Washington, DC 20007

Larry Bird
150 Causeway Street
Boston, MA 02114

George Blanda
P.O. Box 1153
La Quinta, CA 92253

Vida Blue
P.O. Box 14438
Oakland, CA 94614

Wade Boggs
24 Fenway Park
Boston, MA 02215

Brian Boitano
109 Panoramic Way
Berkeley, CA 94704

Manute Bol
P.O. Box 25040
Philadelphia, PA 19147

Bjorn Borg
One Erieview Plaza #1300
Cleveland, OH 44114

Brian Bosworth
5305 Lake Washington Blvd.
Kirkland, WA 98033

Terry Bradshaw
Rt. 1, Box 227
Gordonville, TX 76345

George Brett
P.O. Box 1969
Kansas City, MO 64141

Lou Brock
12595 Durbin Drive
St. Louis, MO 63141

John Brodie
c/o NBC Sports
30 Rockefeller Plaza
New York, NY 10020

Jim Brown
1851 Sunset Plaza Drive
Los Angeles, CA 90069

Jack Buck
c/o CBS Sports
51 W. 52nd Street
New York, NY 10019

Bill Buckner
3 McDonald Circle
Andover, MA 01810

Zola Budd
1 Church Row, Wandsworth Plain,
London, SW18, ENGLAND

Bettina Bunge
c/o USTA
51 E. 42nd Street
New York, NY 10017

Jerry Burns
9520 Viking Drive
Eden Prairie, MN 55344

Dr. Jerry Buss
P.O. Box 10
Inglewood, CA 90306

Dick Butkus
151 El Camino Drive
Beverly Hills, CA 90212

C   C

Hector Camacho
Star Rt., Box 113
Clewiston, FL 33440

Jose Canseco
Oakland-Alameda Coliseum
Oakland, CA 94621

Jennifer Capriati
One Erieview Plaza #1300
Cleveland, OH 44114

Rod Carew
5144 E. Crescent Drive
Anaheim, CA 92807

Peter & Kitty Carruthers
22 E. 71st Street
New York, NY 10021

Bud Carson
Cleveland Stadium
Cleveland, OH 44114

Anthony Carter
9520 Viking Drive
Eden Prairie, MN 55344

Joe Carter
Box 7777, Adelaide Street
Toronto, Ont. MSC 2K7 CANADA

Bill Cartwright
980 N. Michigan Avenue #1600
Chicago, IL 60611

Rosie Casals
1505 Bridgeway #208
Sausalito, CA 94965

Pat Cash
281 Clarence Street
Sydney NSW, 2000, AUSTRALIA

Billy Casper
14 Quiet Meadow Lane
Mapleton, UT 84663

Steve Cauthen
Barry Hills
Lambourne, ENGLAND

Wilt Chamberlain
15216 Antelo Place
Los Angeles, CA 90024

Tom Chambers
2910 N. Central
Phoenix, AZ 85012

Michael Chang
1025 N. Holt Drive
Placentia, CA 92670

Maurice Cheeks
Madison Square Garden
Four Pennsylvania Plaza
New York, NY 10001

Wil Clark
c/o Candlestick Park
San Francisco, CA 94124

Mark Clayton
2269 N.W. 199th Street
Miami, FL 33056

Roger Clemens
24 Fenway Park
Boston, MA 02215

Sebastian Coe
37 Marlborough Road
Sheffield, S. Yorkshire
ENGLAND

Franco Columbu
2947 S. Sepulveda Blvd
Los Angeles, CA 90064

Dennis Conner
401 W. "A" Street #615
San Diego, CA 92101

Jimmy Connors
200 S. Refugio Road
Santa Ynez, CA 93460

Howard Cosell
150 E. 69th Street
New York, NY 10021

Bob Costas
30 Rockefeller Plaza
New York, NY 10020

Robin Cousins
27307 Highway 189
Blue Jay, CA 92317

Bob Cousy
459 Salisbury Street
Worcester, MA 01609

Roger Craig
332 Center Street
El Segundo, CA 90245

Ben Crenshaw
1811 W. 35th Street
Austin, TX 78703

Denny Crum
University of Louisville Basketball
Louisville, KY 40292

Randall Cunningham
c/o Veterans Stadium
Philadelphia, PA 19148

Kevin Curren
5808 Back Court
Austin, TX 78764

Larry Czonka
1940 S.W. 56th
Plantation, FL 33314

D   D

Chuck Daly
c/o The Palace
3777 Lapeer Road
Auburn Hills, MI 48057

Beth Daniel
c/o LPGA
4675 Sweetwater Blvd.
Sugar Land, TX 77479

Ron Darling
19 Woodland Street
Millbury, MA 01527

Brad Daugherty
2923 Streetsboro Road
Richfield, OH 44286

Andre Dawson
c/o Wrigley Field
Chicago, IL 60613

Mary Decker (Slaney)
2923 Flintlock Street
Eugene, OR 97401

Richard Dent
250 N. Washington Road
Lake Forest, IL 60645

Eric Dickerson
P.O. Box 535000
Indianapolis, IN 46253

Dan Dierdorf
c/o ABC Sports
1330 Avenue of Americas
New York, NY 10019

Joe DiMaggio
2150 Beach Street
San Francisco, CA 94123

Mike Ditka
233 W. Ontario
Chicago, IL 60616

Valde Divac
P.O. Box 10
Inglewood, CA 90306

Clyde Drexler
700 N.E. Multnomah Street. #600
Portland, OR 97232

Don Drysdale
1488 Rutherford Drive
Pasadena, CA 91103

Joe Dumars
c/o The Palace
Auburn Hills, MI 48057

Angelo Dundee
1700 Washington Avenue
Miami Beach, FL 33141

Mike Dunleavy
P.O. Box 10
Inglewood, CA 90306

Shawon Dunston
c/o Wrigley Field
Chicago, IL 60613

Mark Duper
2269 N.W. 199th Street
Miami, FL 33056

Roberto Duran
Eleta, Box 157, Arena Colon
Panama City, PANAMA

Leo Durocher
1400 E. Palm Canyon Drive
Palm Springs, CA 92262

Pat Dye
Auburn University Football
Auburn, AL 36849

E   E

Dale Earnhardt
Rt. 8, Box 463
Mooresville, NC 28115

Dennis Eckersley
Oakland-Alameda Coliseum
Oakland, CA 94621

Stefan Edberg
Spinnaregaten 6
S-59300, Vastervik, SWEDEN

Lee Elder
1725 K Street N.W. #1202
Washington, DC 20006

Sean Elliott
P.O. Box 530
San Antonio, TX 78292

John Elway
5700 Logan Street
Denver, CO 80216

Scott Erickson
501 Chicago Avenue South
Minneapolis, MN 55415

Julius Erving
P.O. Box 25040
Philadelphia, PA 19147

Boomer Esiason
200 Riverfront Stadium
Cincinnati, OH 45202

Chris Everett
7100 W. Camino Real #203
Boca Raton, FL 33433

Jim Everett
2327 W. Lincoln Avenue
Anaheim, CA 92801

Patrick Ewing
Madison Square Garden
Four Pennsylvania Plaza
New York, NY 10001

F   F

Nick Faldo
c/o PGA
P.O. Box 12458
Palm Beach Gardens, FL 33410

Tina Ferrari
2901 S. Las Vegas Blvd.
Las Vegas, NV 89109

Cecil Fielder
Tiger Stadium
Detroit, MI 48216

Carlton Fisk
324 W. 35th Street
Chicago, IL 60616

Emerson Fittipaldi
Alameda Amazonas
282 Alphaville Barueri
064500, Sao Paulo, BRAZIL

Cotton Fitzsimmons
2910 N. Central
Phoenix, AZ 85012

Peggy Fleming
16387 Aztec Ridge
Los Gatos, CA 95030

Curt Flood
4139 Cloverdale Avenue
Los Angeles, CA 90008

Raymond Floyd
P.O. Box 12458
Palm Beach Gardens, FL 33410

Doug Flutie
21 Spring Valley Road
Natick, MA 01760

Whitey Ford
38 Schoolhouse Lane
Lake Success, NY 11020

George Foreman
2202 Lone Oak
Houston, TX 77093

A.J. Foyt
6415 Toledo
Houston, TX 77008

Julio Franco
c/o Arlington Stadium
Arlington, TX 76010

Joe Frazier
2917 N. Broad Street
Philadelphia, PA 19132

Walt Frazier
675 Flamingo Drive
Atlanta, GA 30311

G   G

Gary Gaetti
2000 State College Blvd.
Anaheim, CA 92805

Gayle Gardner
c/o NBC Sports
30 Rockefeller Plaza
New York, NY 10020

Randy Gardner
4640 Glencove Avenue #6
Marina Del Rey, CA 90291

Zina Garrison
2665 S. Bay Shore #1002
Miami, FL 33133

Steve Garvey
228 S. Anita
Los Angeles, CA 90049

Mark Gastineau
598 Madison Avenue
New York, NY 10022

Willie Gault
332 Center Street
El Segundo, CA 90245

Vitas Gerulaitas
200 E. End Avenue #15P
New York, NY 10028

Joe Gibbs
13832 Redskin Drive
Herndon, VA 20041

Althea Gibson (Darbeu)
275 Prospect Street #768
East Orange, NJ 07017

Bob Gibson
215 Belleview Blvd. S.
Belleview, NE 68005

Kirk Gibson
1082 Oak Pointe Drive
Pontiac, MI 48054

Frank Gifford
625 Madison Avenue #1200
New York, NY 10022

Jerry Glanville
Suwanee Road at I-85
Suwanee, GA 30174

Tommy Glavine
Suwanee Road at I-85
Suwanee, GA 30174

Dwight Gooden
Roosevelt Ave. & 126th St.
Flushing, NY 11368

Evonne Goolagong (Cawley)
80 Duntroon Avenue
Roseville, NSW, AUSTRALIA

Rich 'Goose' Gossage
10565 Viacha Way
San Diego, CA 92124

Curt Gowdy
9 Pierce Road
Wellesley Hills, MA 02181

Steffi Graff
Luftschiffring 8
D-6835, Bruhl, Germany

Otto Graham
2241 Beneva Terrace
Sarasota, FL 33582

A.C. Green
3900 West Manchester
Inglewood, CA 90306

Wayne Gretzky
14135 Beresford Drive
Los Angeles, CA 90077

Rosie Grier
11656 Montana #301
Los Angeles, CA 90049

Bob Griese
3250 Mary Street
Miami, FL 33133

Ken Griffey, Jr.
Seattle Kingdom
Seattle, WA 98104

Star Guide 1992-1993

Florence Griffith-Joyner
11444 W. Olympic Blvd., 10th Floor
Los Angeles, CA 90064

Kelly Gruber
Box 7777, Adelaide Street
Toronto, Ont. MSC 2K7 CANADA

Pedro Guerrero
250 Stadium Plaza
St. Louis, MO 63102

Ron Guidry
109 Conway
Lafayette, LA 70507

Ozzie Guillen
324 W. 35th Street
Chicago, IL 60616

Greg Gumbel
51 W. 52nd Street
New York, NY 10019

Janet Guthrie
343 E. 30th Street #312N
New York, NY 10016

Tony Gwynn
9949 Friars Road
San Diego, CA 92120

H   H

Jay Haas
c/o PGA
P.O. Box 12458
Palm Beach Gardens, FL 33410

Charles Haley
4949 Centennial Blvd.
Santa Clara, CA 95054

Dorothy Hamill
2331 Century Hill
Los Angeles, CA 90067

Scott Hamilton
General Delivery
Ferndale, NY 19041

Jim Harbaugh
250 N. Washington Road
Lake Forest, IL 60645

Harlem Globetrotters
6121 Santa Monica Blvd.
Los Angeles, CA 90038

Brian Harper
501 Chicago Avenue S.
Minneapolis, MN 55415

Franco Harris
995 Greentree Road
Pittsburgh, PA 15220

Pat Hayden
c/o CBS Sports
51 W. 52nd Street
New York, NY 10019

Bob Hays
6750 LBJ Freeway #1100
Dallas, TX 75240

Tommy Hearns
19600 W. McNichol Street
Detroit, MI 48219

Beth & Eric Heiden
3505 Blackhawk Drive
Madison, WI 53704

Dave Henderson
Oakland-Alameda Coliseum
Oakland, CA 94621

"Hollywood" Henderson
7 Seafield Lane
Westhampton Beach, NY 11978

Rickey Henderson
10561 Englewood Drive
Oakland, CA 94621

Orel Hershiser
1199 Madia Street
Pasadena, CA 91103

Craig Hodger
980 N. Michigan Avenue #1600
Chicago, IL 60611

Ben Hogan
2911 W. Pafford
Ft. Worth, TX 76110

Hulk Hogan
10901 Winnetka Avenue
Chatsworth, CA 91311

Larry Holmes
413 Northampton Street
Easton, PA 18042

Lou Holtz
Univ. of Notre Dame Football
Notre Dame, IN 46556

Evander Holyfield
310 Madison Avenue #804
New York, NY 10017

Chip Hooper
c/o USTA
51 E. 42nd Street
New York, NY 10017

Jeff Hornacek
2910 N. Central
Phoenix, AZ 85012

Jeff Hostetler
Giants Stadium
East Rutherford, NJ 07073

Gordie Howe
32 Plank Avenue
Glastonburg, CT 06033

Kent Hrbek
H.Humphrey Metrodome
Minneapolis, MN 55415

Bobby Hull
15 - 1430 Maroons Road
Winnipeg, Manitoba
R36 0L5, CANADA

Jay Humphries
2910 N. Central
Phoenix, AZ 85012

Jim 'Catfish' Hunter
RR #1, Box 945
Hertford, NC 27944

I_____I

Hale Irwin
P.O. Box 12458
Palm Beach Gardens, FL 33410

Raghib Ismail
Exhibition Stadium
Toronto, Ont., M6K 3C3, CANADA

J_____J

Bo Jackson
16102 Arrow Hwy.
Irwindale, CA 91706

Phil Jackson
980 N. Michigan Avenue #1600
Chicago, IL 60611

Reggie Jackson
22 Yankee Hill
Oakland, CA 94616

Andrea Jaeger
10695 Bardes Court
Largo, FL 33543

Ferguson Jenkins
P.O. Box 275
Blenheim, Ont. CANADA

Bruce Jenner
P.O. Box 655
Malibu, CA 90265

Tommy John
3133 N. 16th Street
Terre Haute, IN 47804

Gordon Johncock
715 S. Fall River Drive
Coldwater, MI 49036

Ben Johnson
2465 Leisure World
Mesa, AZ 85206

Ervin "Magic" Johnson
3900 W. Manchester
Inglewood, CA 90306

Jimmy Johnson
1 Cowboys Parkway
Irving, TX 78063

Kevin Johnson
2910 N. Central
Phoenix, AZ 85012

Michael Jordan
980 N. Michigan Avenue #1600
Chicago, IL 60611

Jackie Joyner-Kersee
20214 Leadwell
Canoga Park, CA 91304

K   K

Al Kaline
945 Timberlake Drive
Bloomfield Hills, MI 48013

Bela Karolyi
17911 Grand Valley Circle
Houston, TX 77090

Gary Kaspurov
c/o Sports & Culture of USSR
Council of Ministers
Moscow, Russia (USSR)

Jim Kelly
One Bill Drive
Orchard Park, NY 14127

Steve Kerr
2910 N. Central
Phoenix, AZ 85012

Jimmy Key
Box 7777, Adelaide Street
Toronto, Ont. MSC 2K7 CANADA

Jeane-Claude Killey
73 Val-d'Isere
FRANCE

Bernard King
Capital Centre
Landover, MD 20785

Betsy King
c/o LPGA
4675 Sweetwater Blvd.
Sugarland, TX 77479

Billie Jean King
One Erieview Plaza #1300
Cleveland, OH 44114

Don King
968 Pinehurst Drive
Las Vegas, NV 89109

Tom Kite
c/o PGA
P.O. Box 12458
Palm Beach Gardens, FL 33410

Franz Klammer
Mooswald 22
A-9712, Friesach, AUSTRIA

Evel Knievel
9960 York Alpha Drive
N. Royalton, OH 44133

Bobby Knight
Indiana University Basketball
Bloomington, IN 47405

Chuck Knox
5305 Lake Washington Blvd.
Kirkland, WA 98033

Bernie Kosar
Cleveland Stadium
Cleveland, OH 44114

Sandy Koufax
P.O. Box BB
Carpenteria, CA 93013

Jack Kramer
231 N. Glenroy Place
Los Angeles, CA 90049

Tommy Kramer
9520 Viking Drive
Eden Prairie, MN 55344

Dave Krieg
5305 Lake Washington Blvd.
Kirkland, WA 98033

Mike Krzyzewski
Duke University Basketball
Durham, NC 27706

Tony Kubek
8323 North Shore Road
Menasha, WI 54252

Bowie Kuhn
320 N. Murray Avenue
Ridgewood, NJ 07450

L   L

Bill Laimbeer
c/o The Palace
Auburn Hills, MI 48057

Jack LaLanne
P.O. Box 1249
Burbank, CA 91507

Donny Lalonde
33 Howard Street
Toronto, Onttario
M4X 1J6, CANADA

Jake LaMotta
400 E. 57th Street
New York, NY 10022

Sean Landeta
Giants Stadium
E. Rutherford, NJ 07073

Bernhard Langer
c/o PGA
P.O. Box 12458
Palm Beach Gardens, FL 33410

Mark Langston
2000 State College Blvd
Anaheim, CA 92806

Barry Larkin
100 Riverfront Stadium.
Cincinnati, OH 45202

Tommy LaSorda
1473 W. Maxzim Avenue
Fullerton, CA 92633

Rod Laver
P.O. Box 4798
Hilton Head, SC 29928

Henri Leconte
c/o USTA
51 E. 42nd Street
New York, NY 10017

Meadowlark Lemon
P.O. Box 398
Sierra Vista, AZ 85635

Ivan Lendl
800 North Street
Greenwich, CT 06830

Nancy Lopez
3203 Country Club Blvd.
Stafford, TX 77477

Sugar Ray Leonard
1505 Brady Court
Mitchellville, MD 20716

Ronnie Lott
332 Center Street
El Segundo, CA 90245

Marv Levy
One Bill Drive
Orchard Park, NY 14127

Greg Louganis
32700 Vista de las Ondas
Malibu, CA 90265

Carl Lewis
1801 Ocean Park Blvd. #112
Santa Monica, CA 90405

Arie Luyendyk
8225 Country Club Place
Indiaanapolis, IN 46224

Reggie Lewis
c/o Boston Garden
Boston, MA 02114

Greg Luzinski
320 Jackson Road
Medford, NJ 08353

Lewis Lipps
300 Stadium Circle
Pittsburgh, PA 15212

Sandy Lyle
P.O. Box 12458
Palm Beach Gardens, FL 33410

Howie Long
26 Strawberry Lane
Rolling Hills, CA 90274

Fred Lynn
24 Haykey Way
Boston, MA 02115

M_____M

John Madden
c/o CBS Sports
51 W. 52nd Street
New York, NY 10019

Katerina Maleeva
2665 S. Bay Shore #1002
Miami, FL 33133

Johnny Majors
Univ. of Tennessee Football
Knoxville, TN 37996

Jeff Malone
1 Harry Truman Drive
Landover, MD 20785

Karl Malone
5 Triad Center #500
Salt Lake City, UT 84180

Moses Malone
100 Techwood Drive N.W.
Atlanta, GA 30303

Hanna Manlikova
Vymolova 8 Prague 5,
15000, CZECHOSLOVAKIA

Danny Manning
3939 S. Figueroa Street
Los Angeles, CA 90037

Mickey Mantle
c/o True, Rohde & McLain
8080 Central Street , 9th Flr.
Dallas, TX 75206

Dan Marino
2269 N.W. 199th Street
Miami, FL 33056

Don Mattingly
RR 5, Box 74
Evansville, IN 47711

Willie Mays
3333 Henry Hudson Parkway
New York, NY 10463

Tim McCarver
1518 Youngford Road
Gladwynne, PA 19035

John McEnroe
23712 Malibu Colony
Malibu, CA 90265

Willie McGee
c/o Candlestick Park
San Francisco, CA 94124

Fred McGriff
9949 Friars Road
San Diego, CA 92120

Mark McGwire
Oakland-Alameda Coliseum
Oakland, CA 94621

Kevin McHale
c/o Boston Garden
Boston, MA 02114

Jim McKay
1330 Ave. of the Americas
New York, NY 10019

Denny McLain
4933 Coventry Parkway
Ft. Wayne, IN 46804

Jim McMahon
c/o Veterans Stadium
Philadelphia, PA 19148

Rick Mears
12101 Castle King Drive
Bakersfield, CA 93309

Miloslav Mecir
51 E. 42nd Street
New York, NY 10017

David Meggett
Giant Stadium
East Rutherford, NJ 07073

Don Meredith
P.O. Box 597
Santa Fe, NM 87504

Al Michaels
c/o ABC Sports
1330 Avenue of Americas
New York, NY 10019

Reggie Miller
300 E. Market Street
Indianapolis, IN 46204

Larry Mize
P.O. Box 12458
Palm Beach Gardens, FL 33410

Paul Molitor
Milwaukee County Stadium
Milwaukee, WI 53214

Earl 'The Pearl' Monroe
113 W. 88th Street
New York, NY 10025

Joe Montana
664 Oak Park Way
Redwood City, CA 94062

Warren Moon
6919 Fannin Street
Houston, TX 77030

Jim Mora
6928 Saints Drive
Metairie, LA 70003

Joe Morgan (Mgn.)
24 Fenway Park
Boston, MA 02215

Alonzo Morning
Georgetown University Basketball
Washington, DC 20057

Jack Morris
501 Chicago Avenue S.
Minneapolis, MN 55415

Willie Mosconi
1804 Prospect Ridge
Hidden Hts., NJ 08035

Edwin Moses
20 Kimberly Circle
Dayton, OH 45408

Manny Mota
Ave. 27 de Febrero #445
Santo Domingo
DOMINICAN REPUBLIC

Jodie Mudd
P.O. Box 12458
Palm Beach Garden, FL 33410

Shirley Muldowney
16755 Parthenia Street #4
Sepulveda, CA 91343

Chris Mullin
Oakland Coliseum Arena
Oakland, CA 94621

Eddie Murray
1000 Elysian Park Avenue
Los Angeles, CA 90012

Brent Musburger
1330 Avenue of Americas
New York, NY 10019

N

N

Joe Namath
300 E. 51st Street #11A
New York, NY 10022

Ille Nastase
107 W. 75th Street #2A
New York, NY 10028

Martina Navratilova
2665 S. Bay Shore #1002
Miami, FL 33133

Byron Nelson
Rt. 2, Fairway Ranch
Roanoke, TX 76262

John Newcome
T-Bar Tennis Ranch
Box 469
New Brauntfets, TX 78130

Jack Nicklaus
11760 U.S. Highway 1 #6
N. Palm Beach, FL 33408

Ray Nitschke
410 Pepper Mint Court
Oneida, WI 54155

Yannick Noah
c/o Proserv, Inc.
888-17th Street N.W.
Washington, DC 20006

Chuck Noll
300 Stadium Circle
Pittsburgh, PA 15212

Greg Norman
P.O. Box 12458
Palm Beach Garden, FL 33410

Ken Norton
16 S. Peck Drive
Laguna Niguel, CA 92677

Diana Nyad
151 E. 86th Street
New York, NY 10028

O

O

Pat O'Brien
c/o CBS Sports
51 W. 52nd Street
New York, NY 10019

Peter O'Malley
1000 Elysian Park Avenue
Los Angeles, CA 90012

Paul Oneill
100 Riverfront Stadium
Cinncinnati, OH 45202

Tom Osburne
University of Nebraska Football
Lincoln, NE 68588

P   P

Billy Packer
c/o CBS Sports
51 W. 52nd Street
New York, NY 10019

Arnold Palmer
P.O. Box 52
Youngstown, PA 15696

Jim Palmer
P.O. Box 145
Brooklandville, MD 21022

Ara Paraseghian
1326 E. Washington Street
South Bend, IN 46601

Dave Parker
4221 Middle Road
Allison Park, PA 15101

Robert Parrish
Boston Garden
Boston, MA 02114

Floyd Patterson
Springtown Road
Box 336
New Paltz, NY 12561

John Paxson
980 N. Michigan Avenue #1600
Chicago, IL 60611

Walter Payton
1251 E. Golf Road
Schaumburg, IL 60195

Pele
75 Rockefeller Plaza
New York, NY 10019

Roger Penske
366 Penske Plaza
Reading, PA 19603

Ray Perkins
One Buccaneer Place
Tampa, FL 33607

Gaylord Perry
R.R. 3, Box 565
Williamtown, NC 27842

Wm. 'Refrigerator' Perry
250 N. Washington Road
Lake Forest, IL 60645

Richard Petty
Rt #3, Box 631
Randleman, NC 27317

Lou Pinella
103 MacIntyre Lane
Allendale, NJ 07401

Scottie Pippen
980 N. Michigan Avenue #1600
Chicago, IL 60611

Gary Player
1 Erie View Plaza #1300
Cleveland, OH 44114

Mark Price
2923 Streetsboro Road
Richfield, OH 44286

Kirby Puckett
501 Chicago Avenue S.
Minneapolis, MN 55415

Q   Q

Carlos Quintana
24 Fenway Park
Boston, MA 02215

Dan Quisenberry
c/o Candlestick Park
San Francisco, CA 94124

R   R

Bobby Rahal
4601 Lyman Drive
Hilliard, OH 43026

Dan Reeves
57 Lincoln Way
Denver, CO 80216

Tim Rains
324 W. 35th Street
Chicago, IL 60616

J.R. Reid
Two First Union Center #2600
Charlotte, NC 28282

Kurt Rambis
2910 N. Central
Phoenix, AZ 85012

Mary Lou Retton
1637 Beverly Road
Fairmont, WV 26554

Ahmad Rashad
30 Rockefeller Plaza #1411
New York, NY 10020

Harold Reynolds
Seattle Kingdom
Seattle, WA 98104

Jeff Reardon
24 Fenway Park
Boston, MA 02215

Jerry Rice
4949 Centennial Blvd.
Santa Clara, CA 95054

Jody Reed
24 Fenway Park
Boston, MA 02215

Cathy Rigby (McCoy)
110 E. Wilshire #200
Fullerton, CA 92632

Bobby Riggs
508 East Avenue
Coronado, CA 92118

Pat Riley
c/o Madison Square Garden
Four Pennsylvania Plaza
New York, NY 10001

Kathy Rinaldi (c/o USTA)
51 E. 42nd Street
New York, NY 10017

Bill Ripken
Memorial Stadium
Baltimore, MD 21218

Cal Ripken, Jr.
Memorial Stadium
Baltimore, MD 21218

Oscar Robertson
6 E. 4th Street
Cincinnati, OH 45202

Brooks Robinson
1506 Sherbrook Road
Lutherville, MD 21093

David Robinson
P.O. Box 530
San Antonio, TX 78292

Eddie Robinson
Grambling Football
Grambling, LA 71245

Frank Robinson
15557 Aqua Verde Drive
Los Angeles, CA 90024

John Robinson
2327 W. Lincoln Avenue
Anaheim, CA 92801

Dennis Rodman
The Palace
Auburn Hills, MI 48057

Bill Rogers
372 Chestnut Hill Avenue
Boston, MA 02146

Pete Rose
9180 Given Road
Cincinnati, OH 45243

Ken Rosewall
111 Pentacost Avenue
Turramurra, NSW
2074, AUSTRALIA

Kyle Rote
1175 York Avenue
New York, NY 10021

Pete Rozelle
410 Park Avenue
New York, NY 10022

Mike Rozier
P.O. Box 1516
Houston, TX 77001

Ravashing Rick Rude
1000 S. Industrial Blvd.
Dallas, TX 75207

Wilma Rudolph
850 N. Meridian Street #102
Indianapolis, IN 46204

Bill Russell
P.O. Box 58
Mercer Island, WA 98040

Jeff Russell
1500 Copeland Road
Arlington, TX 76010

Johnny Rutherford
4919 Black Oak Lane
Ft. Worth, TX 76114

Nolan Ryan
P.O. Box 670
Alvin, TX 77512

S   S

Gabriela Sabatini
2665 S. Bay Shore #1002
Miami, FL 33133

Brett Saberhagen
19229 Arminta Street
Reseda, CA 91335

Chris Sabo
100 Riverfront Stadium
Cincinnati, OH 45202

Alberto Salazar
3968 W. 13th Avenue
Eugene, OR 97402

John Salley
c/o The Palace
Auburn Hills, MI 48057

Pete Sampras
6816 Verde Ridge Road
Rancho Palos Verdes, CA 90274

Ralph Sampson
One Sports Parkway
Sacramento, CA 95834

Ryne Sandberg
c/o Wrigley Field
Chicago, IL 60613

Barry Sanders
1200 Featherstone Road
Pontiac, MI 48057

Deion Sanders
Suwanee Road at I-85
Suwanee, GA 30174

Benito Santiago
Seattle Kingdom
Seattle, WA 98104

Randy Savage
P.O. Box 3859
Stamford, CT 06905

Gale Sayers
624 Buck Road
Northbrook, IL 60062

Bo Schembechler
870 Arlington Blvd.
Ann Arbor, MI 48106

Max Schmeling
2115 Hallenstedt
Hamburg, GERMANY

Mrs. Marge Schott
100 Riverfront Stadium
Cincinnati, OH 45202

Byron Scott
P.O. Box 10
Inglewood, CA 90306

Vin Scully
1555 Capri Drive
Pacific Palisades, CA 90272

Tom Seaver
Larkspur Lane
Greenwich, CT 06830

George Seifert
4949 Centennial Blvd.
Santa Clara, CA 95054

Rony Seikaly
The Miami Arena
Miami, FL 33136

Monica Seles
2665 S. Bay Shore Drive #1002
Miami, FL 33133

Art Shell
30816 rue de la Pierre
Rancho Palos Verdes, CA 90274

Bill Shoemaker
2545 Fairfield Place
San Marino, CA 91108

Pam Shriver
2665 S. Bay Shore Drive #1002
Miami, FL 33133

Don Shula
16220 W. Prestwick Place
Miami Lakes, FL 33014

Ruben Sierra
1500 Copeland Road
Arlington, TX 76010

Phil Simms
Giants Stadium
East Rutherford, NJ 07073

O.J. Simpson
360 Rockingham Avenue
Los Angeles, CA 90049

Dean Smith
U.N.C. Basketball
Chapel Hill, NC 27599

Ozzie Smith
250 Stadium Plaza
St. Louis, MO 63102

Stan Smith
888 - 17th Street N.W. #1200
Washington, DC 20006

J.C. Snead
P.O. Box 1152
Ponte Verde Beach, FL 32082

Sam Snead
P.O. Box 777
Hot Springs, VA 24445

Warren Spahn
Route #2
Hartshorne, OK 74547

Emanuel Stewart
19600 W. McNichol Street
Detroit, MI 48219

Michael Spinks
20284 Archdale
Detroit, MI 48235

Jackie Stewart
24 Rte. de Divonne
1260, Lyon, SWITZERLAND

Mark Spitz
383 Dalehurst
Los Angeles, CA 90024

Payne Stewart
P.O. Box 12458
Palm Beach Gardens, FL 33410

Kenny Stabler
1 St. Louis Street #2004
Mobile, AL 36602

Dick Stockton
715 Stadium Drive
San Antonio, TX 78212

Willie Stargell
7232 Thomas Blvd.
Pittsburgh, PA 15208

John Stockton
5 Triad Center #500
Salt Lake City, UT 84180

Bart Starr
5250 East Onyx
Paradise Valley, AZ 85253

Hank Stram
194 Belle Terre Blvd.
Covington, LA 70483

Roger Staubach
6750 LBJ Freeway
Dallas, TX 75109

Curtis Strange
c/o PGA
P.O. Box 12458
Palm Beach Gardens, FL 33410

Jan Stephenson
6300 Ridglea #1118
Ft. Worth, TX 76116

Darryl Strawberry
4740 Zelzah Avenue
Encino, CA 91316

David Stern
645 - 5th Avenue
New York, NY 10022

Danny Sullivan
201 S. Rockingham Avenue
Los Angeles, CA 90049

Teofilo Stevenson
Comite Olimppicu,
Hotel Havana
Libre, Havana, CUBA

Lynn Swann
5750 Wilshire Blvd. #475W
Los Angeles, CA 90036

T   T

Paul Tagliabue
410 Park Avenue
New York, NY 10022

Roscoe Tanner
1109 Gnome Trail
Lookout Mountain, TN 37350

Jerry Tarkanian
U.N.L.V. Basketball
Las Vegas, NV 89154

Fran Tarkington
3345 Peachtree Road N.E.
Atlanta, GA 30326

Roy Tarpley
777 Sports Street
Dallas, TX 75207

Danny Tartabull
P.O. Box 1969
Kansas City, MO 64141

Lawrence Taylor
Giants Stadium
E. Rutherford, NJ 07073

Vinny Testaverde
One Buccaneer Place
Tampa, FL 33607

Mickey Tettleton
Tiger Stadium
Detroit, MI 48216

Joe Theisman
150 Branch Road S.E.
Vienna, VA 22180

Debi Thomas
22 E. 71st Street
New York, NY 10021

Frank Thomas
324 W. 35th Street
Chicago, IL 60616

Isaiah Thomas
c/o the Palace
Auburn Hills, MI 48057

John Thompson
Georgetown University Basketball
Washington, DC 20057

Mychal Thompson
3900 W. Manchester Blvd.
Los Angeles, CA 90306

Wayman Tisdale
One Sports Parkway
Sacramento, CA 95834

Y.A. Tittle
611 Burleson Street
Marshall, TX 75670

Torvill & Dean
83 Scotland Road
Old Basford Nottingham
Notts. ENGLAND

Alan Trammell
Tiger Stadium
Detroit, MI 48216

Lee Trevino
14901 Quorum Drive #170
Dallas, TX 75240

Bob Tway
P.O. Box 12458
Palm Beach Gardens, FL 33410

Mike Tyson
968 Pinehurst Drive
Las Vegas, NV 89109

U   U

Bob Uecker
60 W. 15734
Menomonee Fall, WI 53051

Johnny Unitas
6254 W. Timonium Road
Lutherville, MD 21093

Al Unser
7625 Central N.W.
Albuquerque, NM 87105

Al Unser, Jr
3243 Calle de Deborah N.W.
Albuquerque, NM 87104

Bobby Unser
7700 Central S.W.
Albuquerque, NM 87105

Gene Upshaw
c/o NFL Players Association
1300 Connecticut Avenue
Washington, DC 20036

V   V

Fernando Valenzuela
3004 N. Beachwood Drive
Los Angeles, CA 90027

Kiki Vandeweghe
Madison Square Garden
New York, NY 10001

Ken Venturi
P.O. Box 12458
Palm Beach Gardens, FL 33410

Guillermo Vilas
Avenue Foch 86
Paris, FRANCE

Faye Vincent
350 Park Avenue
New York, NY 10022

Frank Viola
William A. Shea Stadium
Flushing, NY 11368

W   W

Virginia Wade
Sharstead Court
Sittingbourne, Kent, ENGLAND

Lanny Wadkins
c/o PGA
P.O. Box 12458
Palm Beach Gardens, FL 33410

Greta Waitz
Rovnkollbakken 79
Oslo, 9, NORWAY

Jersey Joe Walcott
1500 Baird Avenue
Camden, NJ 08103

Herschel Walker
9520 Viking Drive
Eden Prairie, MN 55344

Tim Wallach
Olympic Stadium
Montreal,Quebec,
CANADA, H2V 3N7

Bill Walsh
c/o NBC Sports
30 Rockefeller Plaza
New York, NY 10020

Andre Ware
1200 Featherstone Road
Pontiac, MI 48057

Tom Watson
1726 Commerce Towers
Kansas City, MO 64105

Tom Weiskopf
5412 E. Morrison Lane
Paradise Valley, AZ 85253

Mark West
2910 N. Central
Phoenix, AZ 85012

Lou Whitaker
Tiger Stadium
Detroit, MI 48216

Danny White
6116 N. Central Expressway
Dallas, TX 75206

Devon White
Box 7777, Adelaide St. P.O.
Toronto, Ont., MSC 2K7, CANADA

Mats Wilander
Vickersvagen 2
Vaxjo, SWEDEN

Hoyt Wilhelm
P.O. Box 2217
Sarasota, FL 33578

Dominique Wilkins
100 Techwood Drive N.W.
Atlanta, GA 30303

Buck Williams
700 N.E. Multnomah Street. #600
Portland, OR 97232

John "Hot Rod" Williams
The Miami Arena
Miami, FL 33136

Matt Williams
c/o Candlestick Park
San Francisco, CA 94124

Ted Williams
P.O. Box 5127
Clearwater, FL 34618

Mookie Wilson
Box 7777, Adelaide St. P.O.
Toronto, Ont., MSC 2K7, CANADA

Dave Winfield
2050 Center Avenue
Fort Lee, NJ 07024

Katarina Witt
Sektion Eiskunstlauf
Eisstadion DDR - 900
Karl Marx Stadt
Chemnitz, GERMANY

John Wooden
17711 Margate St. #102
Encino, CA 91316

Icky Woods
200 Riverfront Stadium
Cinncinnati, OH 45202

James Worthy
P.O. Box 10
Inglewood, CA 90306

Sam Wyche
200 Riverfront Stadium
Cinncinnati, OH 45202

Y   Y

Caleb Yarborough
c/o NASCR
1801 Volusia Avenue
Daytona Beach, FL 32015

Carl Yastrzemski
4621 S. Ocean Blvd.
Highland Beach, FL 33431

Steve Young
4949 Centennial Blvd.
Santa Clara, CA 95054

Robin Yount
Milwaukee County Stadium
Milwaukee, WI 53214

Z   Z

Don Zimmer
10124 Yacht Club Drive
St. Petersburg, FL 33706

"Fuzzy" Zoeller
c/o PGA
P.O. Box 12458
Palm Beach Gardens, FL 33410

Politics

They're Not A Star Until
They're A Star In Star Guide™

A   A

Bella Abzug
2 Fifth Avenue
New York, NY 10011

King Bhumibol Adulyadey
Villa Chitralada
Bangkok, THAILAND

Spiro T. Agnew
78 Columbia Drive
Rancho Mirage, CA 92270

Sen. Daniel K. Akaka (HI)
Senate Hart Bldg. #720
Washington, DC 20510

Emperor Akihoto
The Imperial Palace
Tokyo, JAPAN

President Hafez Al-Assad
Office of the President
Damascus, SYRIA

Prince Albert of Monaco
Palais De Monace
Boite Postal 518
98015 Monte Carlo, MONACO

Rep. Bill Alexander (AK)
233 Cannon, Hse. Office Bldg.
Washington, DC 20515

Sec. Lamar Alexander
Department of Education
400 Maryland Avenue. S.W.
Washington, DC 20202

Mehmet Ali Agca
Rebibbia Prison
Rome, ITALY

John B. Anderson
Nova University
Center for Study of Law
Ft. Lauderdale, FL 33314

Prince Andrew of England
Sunninghill Park
Windsor, ENGLAND

Princess Anne of England
Gatcombe Park
Gloucestershire, ENGLAND

President Corazon Aquino
Malacanang Palace
Manila, PHILIPPINES

Yassir Arafat
Palais Essada La Marsa
Arnestconseil 17, Belvedere 1004
Tunis, TUNISIA

Rep. Bill Archer (TX)
House Longworth Bldg. #1236
Washington, DC 20515

Moshe Arens
49 Hagderat
Savyon, ISREAL

Rep. Les Aspin (WI)
House Rayburn Bldg. #2336.
Washington, DC 20515

B

B

Ex-Gov. Bruce Babbitt
2095 E. Camelback Road
Phoenix, AZ 85016

Ex-Sen. Howard Baker
P.O. Box 8
Huntsville, TN 37756

Sec. James A. Baker III
Department of State
2201-"C" Street N.W.
Washington, DC 20520

Gov. Nornam Bangerter (UT)
210 State Capitol
Salt Lake City, UT 84114

Abolhassan Bani-Sadre
Auvers-Sur-Oise
FRANCE

Birch Bayh
1575 "I" Street #1025
Washington, DC 20005

Queen Beatrix of Holland
Kasteel Drakesteijn
Lage Vuursche, 3744 BA
HOLLAND

Menachem Begin
One Rosenbaum Street
Tel Aviv, ISRAEL

Sen. Lloyd Bensten (TX)
Senate Hart Bldg. #703
Washington, DC 20510

HRH Prince Bertil
Hertigens av Halland
Kungl Slottet
11130, Stockholm, SWEDEN

Alexander Bessmertnykh
32-34 Somolenskaya
Sennaya Polschachad
Moscow, USSR

Ex-P.M. Benazir Bhutto
70 Clifton Road
Karachi, Pakistan

Sen. Joseph Biden, Jr. (DL)
221 Russel, Sen. Office Bldg.
Washington, DC 20510

Rep. Michael Bilirakis (FL)
House Rayburn Bldg. #2432
Washington, DC 20515

Justice Harry A. Blackmun
U.S. Supreme Court
Washington, DC 20543

Julian Bond
361 W. View Drive
Atlanta, GA 30310

Rep. David Bonior (MI)
House Rayburn Building #2242
Washington, DC 20515

Sen. David Boren (OK)
Senate Russell Building #453
Washington, DC 20510

Ex-Pres. Pieter W. Botha
Pretoria 0001
Republic of SOUTH AFRICA

Sen. Bill Bradley (NJ)
731 Hart Sen. Office Bldg.
Washington, DC 20510

Mayor Tom Bradley
605 S. Irving Blvd.
Los Angeles, CA 90005

Sec. Nicholas Brady
Department of the Treasury
15th St. & Pennsylvania Ave., N.W.
Washington, DC 20220

Hon. Willy Brandt
Erich-Ollenhauser Str. 1
5300, Bonn, 1, GERMANY

Gov. Terry Branstad (IA)
State Capitol
Des Moines, IA 50319

Sen. John Breaux (LA)
Senate Hart Building #516
Washington, DC 20510

Justice William J. Brennan
U.S. Supreme Court
Washington, DC 20543

Rep. George E. Brown (CA)
2300 Rayburn, Hse. Office Bldg.
Washington, DC 20515

Ex-Gov. Jerry Brown
3022 Washington Street
San Francisco, CA 94115

Ron Brown
430 S. Capitol Street SE
Washington, DC 20002

Willie L. Brown, Jr.
State Capitol, Rm #219
Sacramento, CA 95184

Zbigniew Brzezinski
School of Government
Columbia University
New York, NY 10027

Patrick J. Buchanan
1017 Saville Lane
McLean, VA 22101

Sen. Dale Bumpers (AR)
Senate Dirksen Building #229
Washington, DC 20510

Ex-Justice Warren E. Burger
3111 N. Rochester Street
Arlington, VA 22213

Barbara Bush
1600 Pennsylvania Avenue
Washington, DC 20505

President George Bush
1600 Pennsylvania Avenue
Washington, DC 20505

Gatsha Mangosuthu Buthelezi
Private Bag X01 Ulundi 3838
Kwazula, SOUTH AFRICA

Sen. Robert Byrd (WV)
311 Hart, Sen. Office Bldg.
Washington, DC 20510

C   C

Gov. Carroll Campbell Jr. (SC)
State House, Box 11369
Columbia, SC 29211

Gov. Gaston Caperton (WV)
State Capitol
Charleston, WV 25305

King Juan Carlos
Palace De La Carcuela
Madrid, SPAIN

Gov. Arne Carlson (MN)
130 State Capitol
St. Paul, MN 55155

Caroline, Princess of Monaco
La Maison de la Source
St. Reme de Provence FRANCE

Rep. Thomas R. Carpes (DL)
House Cannon Building #131
Washington, DC 20515

Ex-Pres. Jimmy Carter
1 Woodland Drive
Plains, GA 31780

Rosalynn Carter
1 Woodland Drive
Plains, GA 31780

Gov. Robert P. Casey (PA)
225 Main Capitol
Harrisburg, PA 17120

Dr. Fidel Castro
Palacio del Gobierno
Havana, CUBA

Sen. John H. Chafee (RI)
567 Dirksen, Sen. Office Bldg.
Washington, DC 20510

Violeta Chamarrol
Presidential Palace
Managua, NICARAGUA

HRH Prince Charles
Kensington Palace
London, W8, ENGLAND

Cesar Chavez
Box 62,La Paz
Keene, CA 93531

Sec. Dick Cheny
The Pentagon
Washington, DC 20301

Gov. Lawton Chiles (FL)
The Capitol
Tallahassee, FL 32301

President Chaing Ching-Kuo
18 Chang An East Road
Taiwan, REPUBLIC OF CHINA

Shirley Chisholm
Mt. Holyoke College
S. Hadley, MA 01075

Ramsey Clark
36 E. 12th Street
New York, NY 10003

Rep. William Clay (MO)
2470 Rayburn, Hse. Office Bldg.
Washington, DC 20515

Clark Clifford
815 Connecticut Avenue N.W.
Washington, DC 20006

Gov. Bill Clinton (AR)
250 State Capitol
Little Rock, AR 72201

Sen. Dan Coats (IN)
Senate Russell Bldg. #407
Washington, DC 20510

Sen. Thad Cochran (MS)
Senate Russell Building #326
Washington, DC 20510

Ex-Rep. Tony Coelho (CA)
787 - 7th Avenue
New York, NY 10036

Sen. William S. Cohen (ME)
322 Hart, Sen. Office Bldg.
Washington, DC 20510

Rep. Barbara-Rose Collins (MI)
1541 Longworth, Hse. Office Bldg.
Washington, DC 20515

Rep. Cardiss Collins (IL)
2264 Rayburn, Hse. Office Bldg.
Washington, DC 20515

John Connally
P.O. Box 2557
Houston, TX 72252

Sen. Kent Conrad (ND)
Senate Dirksen Building #724
Washington, DC 20510

Ex-King Constantine
4 Linnell Drive
Hampstead Way
London, NW11, ENGLAND

Rep. John Conyers (MI)
2426 Rayburn, Hse. Office Bldg.
Washington, DC 20515

Archibald Cox
Glesen Lane
Weyland, MA 01778

Sen. Larry Craig (ID)
Senate Hart Building #302
Washington, DC 20510

Rep. Phillip Crane (IL)
House Longworth Building 1035
Washington, DC 20515

Sen. Alan Cranston (CA)
112 Hart, Sen. Office Bldg.
Washington, DC 20510

Pres. Alfredo Cristiani
Office of the President
San Salvador, El Salvador

Gov. Mario Cuomo (NY)
State Capitol
Executive Chamber
Albany, NY 12224

D

D

Mayor Richard Daley
City Hall, 5th Floor
121 N. Lasalle Street
Chicago, IL 60602

Sen. Alfonse M. D'Amato (NY)
Senate Hart Building #520
Washington, DC 20510

Sen. John Danforth (MO)
Senate Russell Building #249
Washington, DC 20510

Angela Davis
c/o Ethnic Studies Dept.
San Francisco State University
San Francisco, CA 94132

Sen. Dennis DeConcini (AZ)
Senate Hart Building #328
Washington, DC 20510

Javier Perez de Cuellar
One United Nation Plaza
New York, NY 10017

President W. F. deKlerk
Union Building
Pretoria 0001, South Africa

Rep. Ronald V. Dellums (CA)
2136 Rayburn, Hse. Office Bldg.
Washington, DC 20515

HRH Princess Diana
Kensington Palace
London, W8, ENGLAND

Rep. John Dingell (MI)
2328 Rayburn, Hse. Office Bldg.
Washington, DC 20515

Mayor David Dinkins
City Hall
New York, NY 10003

Sen. Alan Dixon (IL)
Senate Hart Building #331
Washington, DC 20510

Sen. Christopher Dodd (CT)
Senate Russell Building #444
Washington, DC 20510

Sen. Robert Dole (KS)
141 Hart, Sen. Office Bldg.
Washington, DC 20510

Sen. Pete Domenici (NM)
434 Dirksen, Sen. Office Bldg.
Washington, DC 20510

Ex-Gov. Michael Dukakis
85 Perry Street
Brookline, MA 02146

Sen. Dave Durenberger (MN)
Senate Russell Building #154
Washington, DC 20510

Jean-Claude Duvalier
Hotel de l'Abbaye
Talloires, FRANCE

E   E

Gov. Jim Edgar (IL)
Office of the Governor
State House
Springfield, IL 62706

Prince Edward
Buckingham Palace
London, SW1, ENGLAND

Rep. Don Edwards (CA)
House Rayburn Building #2307
Washington, DC 20515

Ex-Gov. Edwin W. Edwards
15919 Highland Road
Baton Rouge, LA 70810

John Ehrlichman
P.O. Box 5559
Santa Fe, NM 87502

David Eisenhower
P.O. Box 278
Kimberton, PA 19442

Julie Nixon-Eisenhower
P.O. Box 278
Kimberton, PA 19442

HRH Queen Elizabeth II
Buckingham Palace
London, SW1, ENGLAND

HRH Elizabeth, Queen Mother
Clarence House
London, SW1, ENGLAND

Pres. Guillermo Endara
Presidential Palace
Panama City, PANAMA

Gov. John Engler (MI)
101 N. Capitol
Lansing, MI 48909

Rep. Mike Espy (MS)
House Cannon Building #216
Washington, DC 20515

Charles Evers
1072 Lynch Street
Jackson, MS 39203

Sen. James Exon (NE)
Senate Hart Building #528
Washington, DC 20510

F   F

King Fahd
Royal Palace
Riyadh, SAUDI ARABIA

Ex-Mayor Dianne Feinstein
30 Presidio Terrace
San Francisco, CA 94118

Geraldine Ferraro
22 Deepdene Road
Forest Hills, NY 11375

Gov. Joan Finney (KS)
State Capitol, 2nd Floor
Topeka, KS 66612

Marlin Fitzwater
Press Secretary
1600 Pennsylvania Avenue
Washington, DC 20500

Rep. Thomas Foley (WA)
House Longworth Building #1201
Washington, DC 20515

Betty Ford
P.O. Box 927
Rancho Mirage, CA 92270

Ex-Pres. Gerald R. Ford
40365 San Dune Road
Rancho Mirage, CA 92270

Sen. Wendell Ford (KY)
Senate Russell Building #173A
Washington, DC 20510

Sen. Wyche Fowler, Jr. (GA)
Senate Russell Building #204
Washington, DC 20515

Rep. Barney Frank (MA)
House Rayburn Building #2404
Washington, DC 20515

Ex-Sen. J. William Fulbright
2527 Belmont Road N.W.
Washington, DC 20005

G   G

Col. Mu' ammar Gaddafi
State Office/Babel Aziziya
Tripoli, LIBYA

Gov. Booth Gardner (WA)
Legislative Building
Olympia, WA 98504

Sen. Jake Garn (UT)
Senate Dirksen Building #505
Washington, DC 20510

Rep. Richard Gephart (MO)
House Longworth Building #1432
Washington, DC 20515

Rep. Newt Gingrich (GA)
House Rayburn Building #2438
Washington, DC 20515

Sen. John Glenn (OH)
Senate Hart Bldg. #503
Washington, DC 20510

Judy Goldsmith
1111 Army-Navy Drive
Arlington, VA 22202

Ex-Sen. Barry Goldwater
6250 Hogahn
Paradise Valley, AZ 85253

Mayor Wilson Goode
City Hall,
Philadelphia, PA 19107

Chmn. Mikhail S. Gorbachev
4 Staraya Ploschad
Moscow, U.S.S.R.

Sen. Albert Gore, Jr. (TN)
Senate Russell Building #393
Washington, DC 20510

Sen. Bob Graham (FL)
Senate Dirksen Building #241
Washington, DC 20510

Sen. Phil Gramm (TX)
Senate Russell Building #370
Washington, DC 20510

Rep. Fred Grandy (IA)
418 Cannon House Building #418
Washington, DC 20515

Alan Greenspan
Federal Reserve System
20th St. & Constitution Ave. NW
Washington, DC 20551

Gov. Judd Gregg (NH)
State House
Concord, NH 03301

H   H

Philip Habib
1606 Courtland Road
Belmont, CA 94002

Gen. Alexander Haig, Jr.
1155 - 15th Street N.W. #800
Washington, DC 20005

H.R. (Bob) Haldeman
443 N. McCadden Place
Los Angeles, CA 90004

Gus Hall
235 W. 23rd Street
New York, NY 10011

Rep. Lee Hamilton (IN)
House Rayburn Building #2187
Washington, DC 20515

Sen. Tom Harkin (IA)
Senate Hart Building #531
Washington, DC 20515

Ex-Sen. Gary Hart
370 - 17th Street, Box 185
Denver, CO 80201

King Hassan II
Royal Palace
Rabat, MOROCCO

Sen. Orrin G. Hatch (UT)
Senate Russell Building #135
Washington, DC 20510

Rep. Charles Hatcher (GA)
2434 Rayburn, Hse. Office Bldg.
Washington, DC 20515

Sen. Mark O. Hatfield (OR) 711 Senate Hart Building Washington, DC 20510	**Benjamin Hooks** 260 - 5th Avenue New York, NY 10001
Ex-Sen. Dr. S.I. Hayakawa P.O. Box 100 Mill Valley, CA 94941	**Rep. Carroll Hubbard, (KY)** Rayburn, Hse. Office Bldg. #2267 Washington, DC 20515
Tom Hayden 10960 Wilshire blvd. #908 Los Angeles, CA 90024	**Hubert H. Humphrey III** 555 Park Street #310 St. Paul, MN 55103
Sen. Howell Heflin (AL) Senate Hart Building #728 Washington, DC 20510	**Gov. Guy Hunt (AL)** 11 South Union Street Montgomery, AL 36130
Sen. Jesse Helms (NC) Senate Dirken Building #403 Washington, DC 20510	**Saddam Hussein** Al-Sijoud Palace Baghdad, IRAQ
Gov. Walter J. Hickel (AK) P.O. Box A Juneau, AK 99811	**King Hussein I** Box 1055 Amman, JORDAN
Sen. Ernest F. Hollings (SC) Russell, Sen. Office Bldg. #125 Washington, DC 20510	**Rep Henry J. Hyde (IL)** Rayburn House Office Bldg. #2262 Washington,. DC 20515

J_____J

Rev. Jesse Jackson 400 "T" Street NW Washington, DC 20001	**Gen. Wojciech Jaruzelski** Ministerstwo Obrony Narodowej ul Klonowa 1 009909, Warsaw, POLAND
John Jacob 500 E. 62nd Street New York, NY 10021	**Lady Bird Johnson** LBJ Ranch Stonewall, TX 78671

Sen. J. Bennet Johnston (LA)
136 Hart, Sen. Office Bldg.
Washington, DC 20510

Vernon Jordan, Jr.
1333 New Hampshire NW #400
Washington, DC 20036

K   K

P.M. Toshiki Kaifu
Office of the Prime Minister
Tokyo, JAPAN

Sen. John F. Kerry (MA)
Senate Russell Building #421
Washington, DC 20510

Sen. Nancy L. Kassebaum (KS)
302 Russell, Sen. Office Bldg.
Washington, DC 20510

Gov. Bruce King (NM)
418 State Capitol
Santa Fe, NM 87503

Sen. Bob Kasten (WI)
Senate Hart Building #110
Washington, DC 20510

Coretta Scott King
234 Sunset Avenue N.W.
Atlanta, GA 30314

Petra Kelly
Bundeshaus-HT 718
D-5300 Bonn, Germany

Lane Kirkland
815 - 16th Street N.W.
Washington, DC 20006

Sec. Jack Kemp
451 - 7th Street S.W.
Washington, DC 20410

Jeane Kirkpatrick
6812 Granby Street
Bethesda, MD 20817

Justice Anthony Kennedy
1 - 1st Street, N.E.
Washington, DC 20543

Dr. Henry Kissinger
435 E. 52nd Street
New York, NY 10022

Rep. Joseph P. Kennedy II (MA)
House Longworth Building #1208
Washington, DC 20515

Ex-Mayor Edward I. Koch
1290 Avenue of the Americas
New York, NY 10104

Sen. Ted Kennedy (MA)
Senate Russell Building #315
Washington, DC 20510

Chancellor Helmut Kohl
Marbacher Strasse II
D-6700, Ludwigshafen
Rhein, GERMANY

Sen. Herbert Kohl (WI)
Senate Hart Building #330
Washington, DC 20510

Mayor Teddy Kollek
22 Jaffa Road
Jerusalem, ISRAEL

L   L

Melvin Laird
1730 Rhode Island Ave. N.W.
Washington, DC 20036

Bert Lance
409 E. Line Street
Calhoun, GA 30701

Pres. Vytatis Landsbergis
Parliment House
Vilnius, LITHUANIA

Rep. Tom Lantos (CA)
House Longworth Building #1526
Washington, DC 20515

Lyndon LaRouche
2110 Center Street East
Rochester, NM 55904

Sen. Frank Lautenberg (NJ)
Senate Hart Building #506
Washington, DC 20510

Rep. Jim Leach (IA)
House Longworth Building #1514
Washington, DC 20515

Sen. Patrick J. Leahy (VT)
Senate Russell Building #433
Washington, DC 20510

Rep. Richard Lehman (CA)
House Longworth Building #1319
Washington, DC 20515

Sen. Carl Levin (MI)
459 Russell, Sen. Office Bldg.
Washington, DC 20510

Rep. John Lewis (GA)
House Cannon Building #329
Washington, DC 20515

G. Gordon Liddy
9113 Sunset Blvd.
Los Angeles, CA 90069

Sen. Joseph I Lieberman (CT)
Senate Hart Building #502
Washington, DC 20510

Premier Li Peng
Office of the Premie
Beijing (Peking)
People Republic of China

Sen. Trent Lott (MS)
Senate Russell Building #487
Washington, DC 20510

Rep. Bill Lowery (CA)
House Rayburn Building #2433
Washington, DC 20515

Sen. Richard Lugar (IN)
Hart, Sen. Office Bldg. #306
Washington, DC 20510

Sec. Manuel Lujan, Jr.
Department Of the Interior
C St. Between 18th & 19th St. SW
Washington, DC 20240

M   M

Sen. Connie Mack (FL)
Senate Hart Building #517
Washington, DC 20510

Sec. Edward Madigan
Dept. of Agriculture
14th & Independence Avenue S.W.
Washington, DC 20250

Charles T. Manatt
4814 Woodway Lane N.W.
Washington, DC 20016

Nelson Mandela
Orlando West,
Soweto, Johannesburg, S. AFRICA

Winnie Mandela
Orlando West,
Soweto, Johannesburg, S. AFRICA

Imelda Marcos
2439 Makiki Drive
Honolulu, HI 96822

Princess Margaret
Kensington Palace
London, N5, ENGLAND

Sec. Lynn Martin
Dept. of Labor
200 Constitution Avenue N.W.
Washington, DC 20210

Sec. Bob Martinez
The White House
National Drug Control Policy
OEOB, Room #176
Washington, DC 20500

Eugene J. McCarthy
1003 Turkey Run Road
McLean, VA 22101

Robert C. McFarlane
3414 Prospect Street N.W
Washington, DC 20007

George McGovern
Friendship Station, Box 5591
Washington, DC 20016

Gov. John McKernan, Jr. (ME)
State House Station #1
Augusta, ME 04333

Robert McNamara
2412 Tracy Place N.W.
Washington, DC 20008

Gov. Ned McWherter (TN)
State Capitol
Nashville, TN 37219

Sen. Howard Metzenbaum (OH)
Russell, Sen. Office Bldg. #140
Washington, DC 20515

Gov. Bob Miller (NV)
State Capitol
Carson City, NV 89710

Gov. Zell Miller (GA)
203 State Capitol
Atlanta, GA 30334

Sen. George Mitchell (ME)
Senate Russell Building #176
Washington, DC 20510

P.M. Francois Mitterand
Palais de l'Elysee
55 et 57 rue de Faubourg
St. Honore, 75008, Paris, FRANCE

Sec. Robert Mosbacher
Department of Commerce
14th St. Between Constitution Ave.
& East Street, N.W.
Washington, DC 20230

Sen. Daniel Moynihan (NY)
Senate Russell Building #464
Washington, DC 20510

President Hosni Mubarak
Royal Palace
Cairo, EGYPT

P.M. Robert G. Mugabe
Office Of the Prime Minister
Munhumutapa Building
Harare, ZIMBABWE

P.M. Brian Mulroney
"Stornoway"
Ottawa, Ontario, CANADA

Ex-Sen. Edmund Muskie
1101 Vermont Avenue N.W.
Washington, DC 20005

N   N

Sen. Don Nickles (OK)
Senate Hart Building #713
Washington, DC 20510

General Manuel A. Noriega
#38699-079
Federal Metro. Correctional Center
1531 N.W. 12th Street
Miami, FL 33125

Ex-Pres. Richard Nixon
577 Chestnut Ridge Road
Woodcliff Lake, NJ 07675

Sen. Sam Nunn (GA)
Dirksen, Sen. Office Bldg. #303
Washington, DC 20510

O   O

Justice Sandra Day O'Connor
1 - 1st Street N.E.
Washington, DC 20543

Thomas "Tip" O'Neill
Cape Cod
Harwich Port, MA 02646

Daniel Ortega Saavedra
Nation Reconstruction
Government
Managua, NICARAGUA

Ex-King Otto of Austria
Hindenburger - Str. 15
8034, Pocking, GERMANY

P   P

Rep. Ron Packard (CA)
House Cannon Building #434
Washington, DC 20515

Sen. Bob Packwood (OR)
Russell, Sen. Office Bldg. #259
Washington, DC 20510

Princess Ashraf Pahlavi
12 Avenue Montaigne
75016, Paris, FRANCE

Reverend Ian Paisley
"The Parsonage"
17 Cyprus Avenue
Belfast, 5T5 SNT
NORTHERN IRELAND

Rep. Leon E. Panetta (CA)
House Cannon Building #339
Washington, DC 20515

Sen. Claiborne Pell (RI)
Russell, Sen. Office Bldg. #335
Washington, DC 20510

Rep. Nancy Pelosi (CA)
House Cannon Building #109
Washington, DC 20515

Shimon Peres
P.O. BOX 3263
10 Hayarkon Street
Tel-Aviv, ISRAEL 63571

Mme. Isabel Peron
Moreto 3
Los Jeronimos
Madrid, SPAIN

HRH Prince Philip
Buckingham Palace
London, ENGLAND

Thomas Pickering
799 United Nation Plaza
New York, NY 10017

General Colin Powell
Joint Chief of Staff
The Pentagon - Room 2E872
Washington, DC 20301

Justice Lewis F. Powell, Jr.
U.S. Supreme Court
Washington, DC 20543

Sen. Larry Pressler (SD)
Hart, Sen. Office Bldg. #133
Washington, DC 20510

Sen. David Pryor (AR)
Senate Russell Building #267
Washington, DC 20510

Rep. Carl D. Pursell (MI)
Longworth, Hse. Office Bldg. #1414
Washington, DC 20515

Q   Q

Vice Pres. Dan Quayle
34th & Massachusetts
Washington, DC 20505

Marily Quayle
34th & Massachusetts
Washington, DC 20505

R   R

Gen. Yitzhak Rabin
The Knesset
Jerusalem, ISRAEL

Gov. Ann Richards (TX)
State Capitol, Box 12428
Austin, TX 78711

Pres. Hashemi Rafsanjani
The Majlis
Teheran, IRAN

Sen. Donald Riegle, Jr. (MI)
Senate Dirkens Building #105
Washington, DC 20510

Rep. Charles B. Rangel (NY)
House Rayburn Building #2252
Washington, DC 20515

Sen. Charles Robb (VA)
Senate Russell Building #493
Washington, DC 20510

Crown Prince Ranier II
Grimaldi Palace
Monte Carlo, MONACO

Gov. Barbara Roberts (OR)
254 State Capitol
Salem, OR 97310

Nancy Reagan
668 St. Cloud Road
Los Angeles, CA 90077

Rev. Pat Robertson
c/o Christian Broadcasting
100 Centerville Turnpike
Virgina Beach, VA 23463

Ex-Pres. Ronald Reagan
668 St. Cloud Road
Los Angeles, CA 90077

Sen. John Rockefeller (WV)
Senate Hart Building #109
Washington, DC 20510

Chief Justice Wm. Rehnquist
U.S. Supreme Court
1 - 1st Street N.E.
Washington, DC 20543

Gov. Roy Romer (CO)
136 State Capitol Building
Denver, CO 80203

Rep. Dan Rostenkowski (IL)
House Rayburn Building #2111
Washington, DC 20515

Sen. Warren Rudman (NH)
Senate Hart Building #530
Washington, DC 20510

S

S

Mme. Jehan El-Sadat
2310 Decatur Place N.W.
Washington, DC 20008

William Sessions
9th St & Pennsylvania Ave. N.W.
Washington, DC 20535

Saltan Hassanal Bokiah
Hassanal Bolkiah Nuda
Bandar Seri Begawan, BRUNEI

P.M. Yitzhak Shamir
Kiriyat Ben Gurian
Jerusalem, 91919, ISREAL

Pres. Oscar Arias Sanchez
CASA Presidencial
San Jose, Costa Rica

Ariel Sharon
The Knesset
Jerusalem, ISRAEL

HRH Sara, Dutchess Of York
Sunninghill Park
Windsor, ENGLAND

Sen. Paul Simon (IL)
Senate Dirkens Building #462
Washington, DC 20510

Justice Antonin Scalia
U.S. Supreme Court
Washington, DC 20543

Sen. Alan Simpson (WY)
Senate Dirkens Building #261
Washington, DC 20510

Mayor Kurt Schmoke
City Hall, 100 Holliday Street
Baltimore, MD 21201

Judge John Sirica
5069 Overlook Road, N.W.
Washington, DC 20016

Rep. Patricia Schroeder (CO)
House Rayburn Building #2208
Washington, DC 20515

Sec. Samuel Skinner
Department of Transportation
400 - 7th Street N.W.
Washington, DC 20590

Gen. Brent Scowcroft
1600 Pennsylvania Avenue
Washington, DC 20500

Eleanor Smeal
3324 Lakeside View Drive
Falls Church, VA 22041

Margaret Chase Smith
Norridgewock Avenue
Skowhegan, ME 04976

Ted Sorenson
345 Park Avenue
New York, NY 10022

Justice David Souter
1 - 1st Street N.E.
Washington, DC 20543

Sen. Arlen Specter (PA)
Senate Hart Building #303
Washington, DC 20510

Princess Stephanie
4725 Forman Avenue
N. Hollywood, CA 91602

Justice John P. Stevens
1 - 1st Street N.E.
Washington, DC 20543

Sen. Ted Stevens (AK)
Senate Hart Building #522
Washington, DC 20510

Rep. Louis Stokes (OH)
Rayburn, Hse. Office Bldg. #2365
Washington, DC 20515

Dr. Louis Sullivan
Dept. Of Health & Human Services
200 Independence Avenue S.W.
Washington, DC 20201

Gov. Mike Sullivan (WY)
State Captitol
Cheyenne, WY 82002

John Sununu
1600 Pennsylvania Avenue
Washington,.DC 20500

Gov. Fife Symington (AZ)
1700 West Washington, 9th Floor
Phoenix, AZ 85007

T   T

Amb. Shirley Temple (Black)
115 Lakeview Drive
Woodside, CA 94062

Hon. Margaret Thatcher
11 Dulwich Gate
London, SE21, ENGLAND

Justice Clarence Thomas
1 - 1st Street N.E.
Washington, DC 20543

Richard Thornburgh
Department of Justice
Constitution Ave. & 10th St. N.W.
Washington, DC 20530

Sen. Strom Thurmond (SC)
Senate Russell Building #217
Washington, DC 20510

Rep. Esteban E. Torres (CA)
Longworth, Office Bldg. #1740
Washington, DC 20515

Pierre Elliot Trudeau
10 Pine Street
Montreal, PQ, CANADA

Bishop Desmond Tutu
Box 31190
Bramfontein, Johannesburg
REPUBLIC OF SOUTH AFRICA

U   U

Rep. Morris K. Udall (AZ)
Cannon, Hse. Office Bldg. #235
Washington, DC 20515

Rep. Fred Upton (MI)
House Longworth Building #1713
Washington, DC 20515

V   V

Cyrus Vance
1 Battery Plaza
New York, NY 10014

Gov. George Voinovich (OH)
Office of the Governor
Columbus, OH 43266

Rep. Guy Vander Jagt (MI)
Rayburn, Hse. Office Bldg. #2409
Washington, DC 20515

Rep. Barbara Vucanovich (NV)
House Cannon Building #206
Washington, DC 20515

W   W

Gov. John Waihee III (HI)
State Capitol
Honolulu, HI 96813

Ex-Gov. George Wallace
P.O. Box 17222
Montgomery, AL 36104

Pres. Kurt Waldheim
Hofburg, Ballhausplatz
1010, Vienna, AUSTRIA

Sen. Malcolm Wallop (WY)
Senate Russell Building #237
Washington, DC 20510

Lech Walesa
Ul Pilotow 17/D3
Gdansk Zaspa, POLAND

Sen. John Warner (VA)
Senate Russell Building #225
Washington, DC 20510

Star Guide 1992-1993   Politics

Sec. James Watkins
Department of Energy
1000 Independence Avenue S.W.
Washington, DC 20585

William H. Webster
9409 Brooke Drive
Bethesda, MD 20817

Gen. William Westmoreland
107 1/2 Tradd St.
Box 1059
Charleston, SC 29401

Justice Byron White
U.S. Supreme Court
Washington, DC 20543

Mayor Kathrine Whitmire
901 Bagby
Houston, TX 77002

Gov. Doug Wilder (VA)
State Capitol
Richmond, VA 33219

Gov. Pete Wilson (CA)
Office of the Governor, State Captol
Sacramento, CA 95814

Sen. Timothy E. Wirth (CO)
Senate Russell Building #380
Washington, DC 20510

Pres. Roh Tae Woo
Office of the President
Seoul, South Korea

Ex-Rep. James Wright, Jr.
#9A10 Lanham Federal Building
819 Taylor Street
Ft. Worth, TX 76102

X _____ X

Chairman Deng Xiaoping
Office of the Chairman
Beijing (Peking)
People Republic of CHINA

Xiang Nan
First Political Commissar
Fujian Military District
People Republic of China

Y-Z _____ Y-Z

Boris Yeltsin
The Kremlin
Moscow, U.S.S.R.

Ex-Mayor Andrew Young
1088 Veltrie Circle S.W.
Atlanta, GA 30311

Mayor Coleman A. Young
Office of Mayor
2 Woodward Avenue
Detroit, MI 48226

Adm. Elmo R. Zumwalt, Jr.
1500 Wilson Blvd.
Arlington, VA 22209

Others

They're Not A Star Until
They're A Star In Star Guide™

A

A

George Abbott
1020 - 5th Avenue
New York, NY 10028

Red Adair
8705 Katy Freeway #302
Houston, TX 77024

Cindy Adams
1050 Fifth Avenue
New York, NY 10028

Richard Adams
26 Church Street
Whitechurch, Hants., ENGLAND

Louis Adler
3969 Villa Costera
Malibu, CA 90265

Sardina Adolpho
36 E. 57th Street
New York, NY 10022

Martin Agronsky
4001 Brandywine Street
Washington, DC 20016

Edward Albee
14 Harrison Street
New York, NY 10013

Dr. Edwin "Buzz" Aldrin
233 Emeral Bay
Laguna Beach, CA 92651

Kim Alexis
111 E. 22nd Street #200
New York, NY 10010

J. Presson Allen
Tophet Road
Roxbury, CT 06783

Hollis Alpert
P.O. Box 142
Shelter Island, NY 11964

Carol Alt
171 E. 84th Street #22E
New York, NY 10028

Robert Altman
128 Central Park South
New York, NY 10019

Rodney Amateau
133 1/2 S. Linden Drive
Beverly Hills, CA 90212

Cleveland Amory
200 W. 57th Street
New York, NY 10019

Wally "Famous" Amos
215 Lanipo Drive
Kailua, HI 96734

Jack Anderson
1531 "P" Street N.W.
Washington, DC 20005

Star Guide 1992-1993   Other Famous People

Maya Angelo
51 Church Street
Boston, MA 02116

Wallis Annenberg
1026 Ridgedale Drive
Beverly Hills, CA 90210

Walter Annenberg
P.O. Box 98
Rancho Mirage, CA 92270

Army Archerd
442 Hilgard Avenue
Los Angeles, CA 90024

Ted Arison
3915 Biscayne Blvd.
Miami, FL 33137

Samuel Z. Arkoff
3205 Oakdell Lane
Studio City, CA 91604

Roone Arledge
535 Park Avenue, #13A
New York, NY 10021

Giorgio Armani
650 - 5th Avenue
New York, NY 10019

Garner Ted Armstrong
P.O. Box 2525
Tyler, TX 75710

Neil Armstrong
1739 N. State Street, Rm. #123
Lebanon, OH 45036

Danny Arnold
1293 Sunset Plaza Drive
Los Angeles, CA 90069

Mary Kay Ash
8787 N. Stemmons Freeway
Dallas, TX 75247

Isaac Asimov
10 W. 66th Street #33A
New York, NY 10023

Sir Richard Attenborough
Old Friars, Richmond Green
Surrey, ENGLAND

B   B

James Bacon
10982 Topeka Drive
Northridge, CA 91324

F. Lee Bailey
66 Long Wharf
Boston, MA 02110

Rev. Jim Bakker
Federal Medical Center
2110 Center Street East
Rochester, MN 55901

Tammy Faye Bakker
P.O. Box 790788
Orlando, FL 32869

161

Bob Banner
2409 Briarcrest Drive
Beverly Hills, CA 90210

Joseph Barbera
3617 Alomar Drive
Sherman Oaks, CA 91403

Dr. Christian Barnard
Waiohal, S. Cross Drive Constantis
Capetown, SOUTH AFRICA

Rona Barrett
1122 Tower Road
Beverly Hills, CA 90210

Mikhail Baryshnikov
35 E. 12th Street #5-D
New York, NY 10003

Robert Bass
201 Main Street
Fort Worth, TX 76102

Alan Bean
26 Sugarberry Circle
Houston, TX 77024

Marilyn Beck
2132 El Roble Lane
Beverly Hills, CA 90210

David Begelman
705 N. Linden Drive
Beverly Hills, CA 90210

Melvin Belli
574 Pacific Avenue
San Francisco, CA 94133

Peter Bencheley
35 Boudinot Street
Princeton, NJ 08540

William Bennett
1150 - 17th Street N.W.
Washington, DC 20036

Ingmar Bergman
P.O. Box 27127
S-10252 Stockholm, SWEDEN

David Berkowitz
c/o Attica State Prison
Attica, NY 14011

Pandro S. Berman
914 N. Roxbury Drive
Beverly Hills, CA 90210

Carl Bernstein
242 E. 62nd Street
New York, NY 10021

Jay Bernstein
9360 Beverly Crest Drive
Beverly Hills, CA 90210

Nina Blanchard
957 N. Cole Avenue
Los Angeles, CA 90028

Bill Blass
444 E. 57th Street
New York, NY 10021

Betsy Bloomingdale
131 Delfern Drive
Los Angeles, CA 90077

Star Guide 1992-1993

Other Famous People

Guion Bluford
LBJ Space Center
Houston, TX 77058

Bob & Ray
420 Lexington Avenue
New York, NY 10021

Peter Bogdanovich
212 Copa de Oro Road
Los Angeles, CA 90077

Erma Bombeck
1703 Redding Road
Fairfield, CT 06430

Yelena Bonner
Uliza Tschakalowa 48
Moscow, USSR

Charley Boorman
Glebe, Annanoe County
Wicklow, IRELAND

William A. Borders
229 W. 43rd Street
New York, NY 10036

Jorge Luis Borges
Maipu 994
Buenos Aires, ARGENTINA

Robert Bork
c/o Amer. Enterprise Institute
1150 - 17th Street N.W.
Washington, DC 20012

Benjamin Bradlee
1717 - 21st Street N.W.
Washington, DC 20009

Christie Brinkley
344 E. 59th Street
New York, NY 10022

Albert "Cubby" Broccoli
809 N. Hillcrest Road
Beverly Hills, CA 90210

Dr. Joyce Brothers
1530 Palisades Avenue
Fort Lee, NJ 07024

Helen Gurley Brown
One West 81st Street #22D
New York, NY 10024

Art Buchwald
1750 Pennsylvania Ave. N.W. #1331
Washington, DC 20006

William F. Buckley, Jr.
150 E. 35th Street
New York, NY 10016

Vincent T. Bugliosi
9300 Wilshire Blvd. #470
Beverly Hills, CA 90210

Anthony Burgess
44 Rue Grimaldi
Monte Carlo, MONACO

Niven Busch
2625 Baker Street
San Francisco, CA 94123

Dick Button
250 W. 57th Street #1818
New York, NY 10107

163

C _____ C

Patrick Caddell
3299 K St. N.W., 5th Floor
Washington, DC 20007

Sarah Caldwell
539 Washington Street
Boston, MA 02111

Joseph Califano
1775 Pennsylvania Avenue N.W.
Washington, DC 20006

Lt. William Calley
c/o V.V. Vicks Jewelry
Cross Country Plaza
Columbus, GA 31903

Stephen Cannell
875 La Loma
Pasadena, CA 91105

Frank Capra
P.O. Box 980
La Quinta, CA 92253

Frank Capra, Jr.
602 South Hudson
Los Angeles, CA 90005

Pierre Cardin
59 Rue du Faubourg
St. Honore
8e, Paris, FRANCE

A.J. Carothers
217 S. Burlingame Avenue
Los Angeles, CA 90049

John Carpenter
8532 Hollywood Blvd.
Los Angeles, CA 90046

Lt. Cmdr. Scott Carpenter
1183 Stradella Road
Los Angeles, CA 90077

Allan Carr
P.O. Box 691670
Los Angeles, CA 90069

Joanna Carson
400 St. Cloud Road
Los Angeles, CA 90077

Hodding Carter III
211 South St. Asaph
Alexandria, VA 22314

Barbara Cartland
Camfield Place Hatfield
Hertfordshire, ENGLAND

Kellye Cash
1325 Boardwalk
Atlantic City, NJ 08401

Oleg Cassini
135 East 19th Street
New York, NY 10019

Engene Cernan
900 Town & Country Lane #210
Houston, TX 77024

Star Guide 1992-1993

Other Famous People

Suzette Charles
1930 Century Park West #403
Los Angeles, CA 90067

Julia Child
125 Western Avenue
Boston, MA 02134

Raymond Chow
23 Baker Road
Craigside Mansion #5B
Hong Kong, B.C.C.

Michael Cimino
9015 Alto Cedro
Beverly Hills, CA 90210

Liz Claiborne
300 E. 56th Street
New York, NY 10022

James Clavell
2006 Thayer Avenue
Los Angeles, CA 90025

Jackie Collins
710 N. Foothill Road
Beverly Hills, CA 90210

Marva Collins
4146 W. Chicago Avenue
Chicago, IL 60651

Michael Collins
4206 - 48th Place N.W.
Washington, DC 20016

Charles (Chuck) Colson
P.O. Box 40562
Washington, DC 20016

Capt. Charles T. Conrad, Jr.
5301 Bolsa Avenue
Huntington Beach, CA 92647

Christian Conrad
15301 Ventura Blvd. #345
Sherman Oaks, CA 91403

Paul Conrad
28649 Crestridge Road
Palos Verdes, CA 90274

Alistair Cooke
Nassau Point
Cutchogue, NY 11935

Dr. Denton Cooley
3014 Del Monte Drive
Houston, TX 77019

Lt. Col. L. Gordon Cooper
5011 Woodley Avenue
Encino, CA 91436

William Coors
c/o Adolph Coors Co.
Golden, CO 80401

David Copperfield
2181 Broadview Terrace
Los Angeles, CA 90068

Francis Coppola
916 Kearny Street
San Francisco, CA 91433

Roger Corman
11611 San Vincente Blvd.
Los Angeles, CA 90049

Norman Corwin
1840 Fairburn Avenue #302
Los Angeles, CA 90025

Jaques Cousteau
425 E. 52nd Street
New York, NY 10022

Mrs. Gertrude Crain
740 N. Rush Street
Chicago, IL 60611

Judith Crist
180 Riverside Drive
New York, NY 10024

D   D

The Dalai Lama
Thekchen Choling
McLeod Gundi, Kangra
Himachal Pradesh, INDIA

Abby Dalton
10000 Santa Monica Blvd. #305
Los Angeles, CA 90067

Margaret Truman Daniel
830 Park Avenue
New York, NY 10028

Nicholas Daniloff
c/o USN & WR
2400 N. Street N.W.
Washington, DC 20037

Altovise (Mrs. Sammy) Davis
1151 Summit Drive
Beverly Hills, CA 90210

John Dean
9496 Rembert Lane
Beverly Hills, CA 90210

Hubert De Givenchy
3 Avenue George V
75008, Paris, FRANCE

Oscar De La Renta
Brook Hill Farm
Skiff Mountain Road
Kent, CT 06757

Dino De Laurentiis
Via Poutina Ku 23270
Rome, ITALY

John Z. DeLorean
834 Fifth Avenue
New York, NY 10028

Agnes DeMille
25 East 9th Street
New York, NY 10003

Brian De Palma
25 Fifth Avenue #4A
New York, NY 10003

John Derek
3625 Roblar
Santa Ynez, CA 93460

Dr. William DeVries
Humana Heart Institute
One Audibon Plaza Drive
Louisville, KY 40201

Star Guide 1992-1993

Barry Diller
1940 Coldwater Canyon
Beverly Hills, CA 90210

Jeanne Dixon
1225 Connecticut NW #411
Washington, DC 20036

Roy Disney
4300 Arcola Avenue
Toluca Lake, CA 91602

Sam Donaldson
1717 DeSales N.W.
Washington, DC 20036

Ivan Dixon
3432 N. Marengo Avenue
Altadena, CA 91101

Gen. James Doolittle
8545 Carmel Valley Road #28A
Carmel, CA 93923

E   E

Blake Edwards
P.O. Box 666
Beverly Hills, CA 90213

Michael Eisner
500 S. Buena Vista
Burbank, CA 91521

John Eisenhower
12333 Wooded Way
Westchester, PA 19380

Linda Ellerbee
17 St. Lukes Place
New York, NY 10014

F   F

Max Factor
9777 Wilshire Blvd. #1015
Beverly Hills, CA 90212

Jules Feiffer
325 West End Avenue
New York, NY 10023

Rev. Jerry Falwell
P.O. Box 1111
Lynchbury, VA 24505

Fedrico Fellini
141A Via Margutta 110
Rome, ITALY

Min. Louis Farrakhan
813 E. Broadway
Phoenix, AZ 85001

Cristina Ferrare
1280 Stone Canyon Road
Los Angeles, CA 90077

Other Famous People

Larry Flynt
9211 Robin Drive
Los Angeles, CA 90069

Charlotte Ford
25 Sutton Place
New York, NY 10023

Eileen Otte Ford
344 E. 59th Street
New York, NY 10022

Milos Forman
The Hampshire House
150 Central Park Square
New York, NY 10019

Bill Forsythe
20 Winton Drive
Glasgow, G12, SCOTLAND

John Fowles
52 Floral Street
London, WC2, ENGLAND

Douglas Fraser
800 E. Jefferson Street
Detroit, MI 48214

Betty Friedan
One Lincoln Plaza
New York, NY 10023

William Friedkin
7471 Woodrow Wilson Drive
Los Angeles, CA 90046

Milton Friedman
Quadrangle Office
Hoover Institute
Stanford University
Palo Alto, CA 94305

Lynette "Squeaky" Fromme
Reformatory for Women
Alderson, WV 24910

Betty Furness
30 Rockefeller Plaza
New York, NY 10112

G _____ G

John Kenneth Galbraith
30 Francis Avenue
Cambridge, MA 02138

Dr. Robert Gale
UCLA Medical Center
Dept. of Medicine, Room 42-121
Los Angeles, CA 90024

Ernest Gallo
600 Yosemite Blvd.
Modesto, CA 95354

Dr. George Gallup II
The Great Road
Princeton, NJ 08540

Wally George
14155 Magnolia Blvd. #127
Sherman Oaks, CA 91423

Mrs. J. Paul Getty
1535 N. Beverly Drive
Beverly Hills, CA 90210

Star Guide 1992-1993

Other Famous People

Allen Ginsberg
Box 582, Stuyvesant Station
New York, NY 10009

Alexander Godinov
8787 Shoreham Drive #1001
Los Angeles, CA 90069

William Golding
Ebble Thatch Bowerchalke
Wiltshire, ENGLAND

William Goldman
740 Park Avenue
New York, NY 10021

Samuel Goldwyn, Jr.
10203 Santa Monica Blvd. #500
Los Angeles, CA 90067

Ellen Goodman
c/o Boston Globe
Boston, MA 02102

Mark Goodson
375 Park Avenue
New York, NY 10022

Lord Lew Grade
3 Audley Square
London, W1Y 5DR, ENGLAND

Rev. Billy Graham
1300 Harmon Place
Minneapolis, MN 55408

Katherine Graham
2920 "R" Street N.W.
Washington, DC 20007

Mrs. Barbara (Cary) Grant
9966 Beverly Grove Drive
Beverly Hills, CA 90210

Earl G. Graves
130 Fifth Avenue
New York, NY 10011

Ex-Rep. William Gray III
500 East 62nd Street
New York, NY 10021

Bob Greene
c/o Chicago Tribune
435 N. Michigan Avenue
Chicago, IL 60611

Dick Gregory
P.O. Box 3266
Tower Hill Farm
Plymouth, MA 02361

Merv Griffin
603 N. Doheny Road
Beverly Hills, CA 90210

Matt Groening
15205 Friends Street
Pacific Palisades, CA 90272

Aldo Gucci
8 Via Condotti
00187, Rome, ITALY

Bob Guccione
1965 Broadway
New York, NY 10023

Cathy Guisewite
c/o Universal Press
4900 Main Street
Kansas City, MO 64112

H   H

Jessica Hahn
P.O. Box 54972
Phoenix, AZ 85078

Arthur Hailey
Box N7776, Lyford Cay
Nassau, BAHAMAS

Alex Haley
P.O. Box 3338
Beverly Hills, CA 90213

Jack Haley, Jr.
1443 Devlin Drive
Los Angeles, CA 90069

Fawn Hall
8339 Chapel Lake Court
Annandale, VA 22003

Jerry Hall
2 Munro Terrace
London, SW10 0DL, ENGLAND

Mrs. Jean Harris
Bedford Hills
Correctional Facility
Bedford Hills, NY 10507

Johnny Hart
c/o News AM Syndicate
1703 Kaiser Avenue
Irvine, CA 92714

Paul Harvey
1035 Park Avenue
River Forest, IL 60305

Eugene Hasenfuss
Marinette, WI 54143

Patricia Hearst
110 - 5th Street
San Francisco, CA 94103

Randolph Hearst, Jr.
959 - 8th Avenue
New York, NY 10019

Mrs. Wm. Randolph Hearst
875 Comstock Avenue #16B
Los Angeles, CA 90024

Christie Hefner
10236 Charing Cross Road
Los Angeles, CA 90024

Hugh Hefner
10236 Charing Cross Road
Los Angeles, CA 90024

Leona Helmsley
36 Central Park Square
New York, NY 10019

Werner Herzog
Karl - Theodor - Street 18
D-8000 40 Munich GERMANY

Don Hewitt
220 Central Park South
New York, NY 10019

Star Guide 1992-1993

Other Famous People

William Hewlett
1501 Page Mill Road
Palo Alto, CA 94304

Tor Heyerdahl
Hulen Meadows
Ketchum, ID 83340

Jack Higgins
Septembertide
Mont DeLa Rocque
Jersey, Channel Islands (U.K.)

George Roy Hill
75 Rockefeller Plaza #700
New York, NY 10019

Sir Edmund Hillary
278A Remuera Road
Auckland, SE2, NEW ZEALAND

Baron Hilton
28775 Sea Ranch Way
Malibu, CA 90265

Kimberly Beck Hilton
28775 Sea Ranch Way
Malibu, CA 90265

John Hinckley, Jr.
St. Elizabeth's Hospital
2700 Martin L. King Avenue
Washington, DC 20005

Shere Hite
P.O. Box 5282, FDR Station
New York, NY 10022

David Horowitz
P.O. Box 49915
Los Angeles, CA 90049

Rev. Rex Humbard
2690 State Road
Cuyahoga Falls, OH 44421

E. Howard Hunt
1245 N.E. 85th Street
Miami, FL 33138

Ray Hunt
1401 Elm Street
Dallas, TX 75202

Joe Hyams
1250 S. Beverly Glen #108
Los Angeles, CA 90024

I   I

Lee Iacocca
571 Edgemere Court
Bloomfield Hills, MI 48013

Carl C. Icahn
1370 Avenue of Americas
New York, NY 10019

Rev. Ike
4140 Broadway
New York, NY 10004

Carlo Imperato
6120 Cartwright
North Hollywood, CA 91606

171

J _____ J

Bianca Jagger
530 Park Avenue #18D
New York, NY 10021

Dr. Robert Jarvik
124 W. 60th Street
New York, NY 10023

Norman Jewison
23752 Malibu Road
Malibu, CA 90265

Joyce Jillson
64 E. Concord Street
Orlando, FL 32801

Steve Jobs
900 Chesapeake Drive
Redwood City, CA 94063

John H. Johnson
820 S. Michigan Avenue
Chicago, IL 60605

K _____ K

Yousuf Karsh
18 E. 62nd Street
New York, NY 10003

Lawrence Kasdan
708 N. Elm Drive
Beverly Hills, CA 90210

Caroline Kennedy-Schlossberg
20 W. 20th Street, 10th Floor
New York, NY 10011

Ethel Kennedy
1147 Chain Bridge Road
McLean, VA 22101

Joan Kennedy
P.O. Box 8642
Boston, MA 02114

John Kennedy, Jr.
1041 - 5th Avenue
New York, NY 10028

Leon Isaac Kennedy
P.O. Box 361039
Los Angeles, CA 90036

Rose Fitzgerald Kennedy
The Compound
Hyannis, MA 02647

Ted Kennedy, Jr.
636 Chain Bridge Road
McLean, VA 22101

Ted Key
1694 Glenhardie Road
Wayne, PA 19087

Star Guide 1992-1993

Other Famous People

Adnan Khashoggi
Box 6, Triad Holding Co.
Riyadh, SAUDI ARABIA

Dr. C. Everett Koop
1350 Avenue of Americas
New York, NY 10019

Victor K. Kiam II
60 Main Street
Bridgeport, CT 06602

Stanley Kramer
12386 Ridge Circle
Los Angeles, CA 90049

James L. Kilpatrick
White Walnut Road
Woodville, VA 22749

Kreskin
201A N. Robertson Blvd.
Beverly Hills, CA 90211

Stephen King
49 Florida Avenue
Bangor, ME 04401

Mathilde Krim
40 W. 57th Street
New York, NY 10019

Gelsey Kirkland
945 Fifth Avenue
New York, NY 10021

Mrs. Joan Kroc
8939 Villa La Jolla Drive
La Jolla, CA 92037

Calvin Klein
205 W. 39th Street
New York, NY 10018

Charles Kuralt
524 W. 57th Street
New York, NY 10019

L   L

Dr. Arthur Laffer
608 Silver Spur Road #229
Rolling Hills Est., CA 90274

Sherry Lansing
5555 Melrose Avenue
Los Angeles, CA 90038

Ann Landers
435 N. Michigan Avenue
Chicago, IL 60611

Ring Lardner, Jr.
55 Central Park West
New York, NY 10023

John Landis
100 Universal City Plaza
Universal City, CA 91608

Gary Larson
4900 Main Street #900
Kansas City, MO 62114

173

Fred Lasswell
1111 N. Westshore Blvd. 604
Tampa, FL 33607

Estee Lauder
767 Fifth Avenue
New York, NY 10022

Ralph Lauren
550 - 7th Avenue
New York, NY 10021

Arthur Laurents
P.O. Box 582
Quoque, NY 11959

Irving Lazar
1840 Carla Ridge
Beverly Hills, CA 90210

Norman Lear
1800 Central Park East
Los Angeles, CA 90067

Dr. Timothy Leary
10106 Sunbrook
Beverly Hills, CA 90210

John Le Carre
Tregiffian, St. Buryan
Penzance, Cornwall, ENGLAND

Spike Lee
40 Acres & A Mule Film Works
124 De Kalb Avenue #2
Brooklyn, NY 11217

Samuel J. Lefrak
97-77 Queen Blvd.
Forest Hills, NY 11374

Sheldon Leonard
1141 Loma Vista Drive
Beverly Hills, CA 90210

Doris Lessing
24 Gondar Gardens
London, NW6, ENGLAND

Ira Levin
40 E. 49th Street
New York, NY 10017

Flora Lewis
NY Times Foreign News
229 W. 43rd Street
New York, NY 10036

Reginald Lewis
TCL Group
99 Wall Street
New York, NY 10005

Arthur L. Liman
345 Park Avenue
New York, NY 10154

Ann Morrow Lindbergh
Scotts Cove
Darien, CT 06820

Frank Lorenzo
333 Clay Street
Houston, TX 77002

James A. Lovell
5725 E. River Road
Chicago, IL 60611

George Lucas
3270 Kerner Blvd. Box 2009
San Rafael, CA 94912

Robert Ludlum
c/o Henry Morrison
56 W. 10th Street
New York, NY 10011

Sidney Lumet
1380 Lexington Avenue
New York, NY 10028

M   M

Jeff MacNelly
Tribune Media Services
720 N. Orange Avenue
Orlando, FL 32801

Norman Mailer
142 Columbia Heights
Brooklyn, NY 11201

Louis Malle
Le Covel
46260 Limogne
En Quercy FRANCE

William Manchester
Westleyan Station
P.O. Box 329
Middleton, CT 06457

Charles Manson
Corcoran Prison
San Joaquin, CA 93660

Marcel Marceau
15 Avenue Montaigne
75008, Paris, FRANCE

Gabriel Garcia Marquez
Fuego 144
Pedregal de San Angel
Mexico City, D.F., MEXICO

Mrs. Alice S. Marriott
4500 Garfield Street
Washington, DC 20007

Forrest Mars
6885 Elm Street
McLean, VA 22101

Garry Marshall
10067 Riverside Drive
Toluca Lake, CA 91602

Masters & Johnson
3530 Camino Del Rio North
San Diego, CA 92108

Robert Maxwell
Headington Hill Hall
Oxford, 0X3 0BB, ENGLAND

Cordelia Scaife May
3 Gateway Center, 6 North
Pittsburgh, PA 15213

Paul Mazursky
16 E. 11th Street #3A
New York, NY 10003

Rod McKuen
1155 Angelo Drive
Beverly Hills, CA 90210

Terrence McNally
218 W. 10th Street
New York, NY 10014

Star Guide 1992-1993

Other Famous People

Edwin Meese III
1075 Springhill Road
McLean, VA 22102

Rolf Mengele
Rotlaustrasse 12
7800, Freiburg, GERMANY

Sue Mengers
2222 Ave. of the Stars #506
Los Angeles, CA 90067

Russ Meyer
3121 Arrowhead Drive
Los Angeles, CA 90068

Lorne Michaels
88 Central Park West
New York, NY 10023

James A. Michener
Pipersville, Box 125
Tinicum, PA 18947

John Milius
888 Linda Flora
Los Angeles, CA 90027

Michael Milken
4543 Tara Drive
Encino, CA 91436

Arthur Miller
RR 1, Box 320 - Tophet Road
Roxbury, CT 06783

Roger Milliken
P.O. Box 3167
Spartanburg, SC 29304

Marvin Mitchelson
1801 Century Park E. #1900
Los Angeles, CA 90067

Thomas L. Monaghan
3001 Earhart
Ann Arbor, MI 48106

Rev. Sun Myung Moon
4 W. 43rd Street
New York, NY 10010

Sara Jane Moore
Federal Ref. for Women
Alderson, WV 24910

Mother Delores (Debra Hart)
Regina Laudis Convent
Bethlehem, CT 06751

Stewart Mott
515 Madison Avenue
New York, NY 10022

Malcolm Muggeridge
Park Cottage
Robertsbridge, Sussex, ENGLAND

Wallace Muhammad
7351 S. Stony Island
Chicago, IL 60617

Rupert Murdoch
660 White Plains Road
Tarrytown, NY 10591

Russell Myers
Tribune Media Service
770 N. Orange Avenue
Orlando, FL 32801

N   N

Ralph Nader
P.O. Box 19367
Washington, DC 20036

Dr. George Nichopoulos
1734 Madison
Memphis, TN 37104

Hal Needham
2220 Avenue of the Stars #302
Los Angeles, CA 90067

A.C. Nielson
Nielsen Plaza
Northbrook, IL 60062

LeRoy Neiman
One W. 67th Street
New York, NY 10023

Dr. Thomas Noguchi
1135 Arlington
Los Angeles, CA 90019

Samuel I. Newhouse, Jr.
950 Fingerboard Road
Staten Island, NY 10305

Oliver North
703 Kentland Drive
Great Falls, VA 22066

O   O

Madalyn Murray O'Hara
2210 Hancock Drive
Austin, TX 78756

John Osbourne
162 Wardour Street
London, W1, ENGLAND

Sydner Omarr
201 Ocean Avenue #17068
Santa Monica, CA 90402

Charles Osgood
c/o CBS
51 W. 52nd Street
New York, NY 10019

Jacqueline Onassis
1040 Fifth Avenue
New York, NY 10028 ✝

Earl Owensby
P.O. Box 184
Shelby, NC 28150

Yuri Orlov
Cornell University
Newman Laboratory
Ithaca, NY 14853

Frank Oz
117 E. 69th Street
New York, NY 10024

P   P

Rosa Parks
305 Federal Building
231 W. Lafeyette
Detroit, MI 48226

Dr. Norman Vincent Peale
1025 Fifth Avenue
New York, NY 10028

I.M. Pei
600 Madison Avenue
New York, NY 10022

H. Ross Perot
12377 Merit Drive
Dallas, TX 75251

T. Boone Pickens
P.O. Box 2009
Amarillo, TX 79198

Roman Polanski
43 Avenue Montaigne
75008, Paris, FRANCE

Sidney Pollack
13525 Lucca Drive
Pacific Palisades, CA 90272

Jonathan Pollard
Federal Reformatory
Marion, IL 62959

Pope John Paul II
Palazzo Apostolico Vaticano
Vatican City, ITALY

Dr. Alvin Poussaint
J. Baker Guidance Center
295 Longwood Avenue
Boston, MA 02115

Mario Puzo
866 Manor Lane
Bay Shore, NY 11706

Monty Python
20 Fitzroy Square
London, W1P 6BB, ENGLAND

R   R

Ron Reagan, Jr.
1283 Devon Avenue
Los Angeles, CA 90024

Orville Redenbacher
1780 Avenida del Mundo #704
Coronado, CA 92118

Rex Reed
1 W. 72nd Street #86
New York, NY 10023

Donald T. Regan
1 Pennsylvania Plaza #2400
New York, NY 10119

Donna Rice
1204 Ina Lane
McLean, VA 22102

Dr. Renee Richards
1604 Union Street
San Francisco, CA 94123

Dr. Sally Ride
LBJ Space Center,
Mail Code: CB
Houston, TX 77058

Hal Roach
1183 Stradella Road
Los Angeles, CA 90077

Harold Robbins
990 North Patencio
Palm Springs, CA 92262

Oral Roberts
7777 Lewis Street
Tulsa, OK 74130

David Rockefeller, Jr.
30 Rockefeller Plaza #506
New York, NY 10112

Mrs. Nelson Rockefeller
812 Fifth Avenue
New York, NY 10024

Gene Roddenberry
10615 Bellagio Road
Los Angeles, CA 90077

Carl T. Rowan
3251-C Sutton Place N.W.
Washington, DC 20016

Mike Royko
435 N. Michigan Avenue
Chicago, IL 60611

Erno Rubik
Magvar Iparmuveszeti
Foisgola, 1121 Budapesit
Zugligetiue, 11/25, HUNGARY

Salman Rushdie
c/o Viking Penguin
40 West 23rd Street
New York, NY 10010

Mark Russell
2800 Wisconsin Avenue #810
Washington, DC 20007

S   S

William Safire
6200 Elmwood Road
Chevy Chase, MD 20815

Carl Sagan
Space Science Bldg.
Cornell University
Ithaca, NY 14853

J.D. Salinger
R.R. #3, Box 176
Cornish Flat, NH 03746

Pierre Salinger
7 Carburton Street
London, W1P 7DT, ENGLAND

Other Famous People

Dr. Jonas Salk
2444 Ellentown Road
La Jolla, CA 92037

Vincent Sardi, Jr.
234 W. 44th Street
New York, NY 10036

Beverly Sassoon
738 S. Holmby Avenue
Los Angeles, CA 90024

Vidal Sassoon
2132 Century Park Lane #108
Los Angeles, CA 90067

Francesco Scavullo
216 E. 63rd Street
New York, NY 10021

Walter M. Schirra, Jr.
P.O. Box 73
Rancho Santa Fe, CA 92067

Arthur Schlesinger, Jr.
33 W. 42nd Street
New York, NY 10036

Daniel Schorr
3113 Woodley Road
Washington, DC 20008

Dr. Robert Schuller
464 S. Esplanade
Orange, CA 92669

George Schultz
Hoover Institute
Stanford University
Palo Alto, CA 94305

Gen. Norman Schwarzkopf
U.S. Central Command
MacDill A.F.B., FL 33608

Martin Scorsese
146 W. 57th Street #75B
New York, NY 10019

John Sculley
20525 Mariani Avenue
Cupertino, CA 95014

Gen. Richard Secord
1 Pennsylvania Plaza #2400
New York, NY 10119

Erich Segal
53 the Pryors
East Heath Road
London, NW3 1BP, ENGLAND

Dr. Seuss (Ted Geisel)
7301 Encelia Drive
San Diego, CA 92037

Sidney Sheldon
10250 Sunset Blvd.
Los Angeles, CA 90077

Adm. Alan Shepard, Jr.
3435 Westheimer Road #1105
Houston, TX 77027

William L. Shirer
P.O. Box 487
Lenox, MA 02140

Hugh Sidey
1050 Connecticut Avenue
Washington, DC 20036

Star Guide 1992-1993

Other Famous People

Fred Silverman
101 Central Park W. #10E
New York, NY 10023

Aaron Spelling
594 N. Mapleton Drive
Los Angeles, CA 90077

Richard Simmons
1350 Belfast
Los Angeles, CA 90069

Steven Spielberg
P.O. Box 6190
Malibu, CA 90264

Neil Simon
10100 Santa Monica Blvd. #496
Los Angeles, CA 90067

Mickey Spillane
c/o General Delivery
Marrells Inlet, SC 22117

Roger Simon
c/o Baltimore Sun
Calvert & Centre Street
Baltimore, MO 21278

Danielle Steel
P.O. Box 1637
Murry Hill Station
New York, NY 10156

Sinbad
20061 Merriday Street
Chatsworth, CA 91311

Gloria Steinem
118 E. 73rd Street
New York, NY 10021

Donald "Deke" Slayton
7015 Gulf Freeway #140
Houston, TX 77087

David Stockman
One New York Plaza
New York, NY 10004

Curtis Sliwa
982 E. 89th Street
Brooklyn, NY 11236

Oliver Stone
321 Hampton Drive #105
Venice, CA 90291

Yako Smirnoff
1132 Napoli
Pacific Palisades, CA 90272

Tom Stoppard
91 Regent Street
London, WC1 4AE, ENGLAND

Liz Smith
160 E. 38th Street
New York, NY 10016

Jimmy Swaggert
P.O. Box 2550
Baton Rouge, LA 70821

Jimmy "The Greek" Snyder
870 - 7th Avenue #2049
New York, NY 10019

John Cameron Swayze
491 Riversville Road
Greenwich, CT 06830

181

T   T

Gay Talese
154 E. Atlantic Blvd.
Ocean City, NJ 08226

Brandon Tartikoff
1479 Lindacrest Drive
Beverly Hills, CA 90210

Mother Teresa
Mission of Charity
54-A Lower Circular Road
Calcutta, 7000016, INDIA

Studs Terkel
850 W. Castlewood
Chicago, IL 60640

Helen Thomas
2501 Calvert Street N.W.
Washington, DC 20008

Cheryl Tiegs
9219 Flicker Way
Los Angeles, CA 90069

Grant Tinker
531 Barnaby Road
Los Angeles, CA 90077

Laurence Tisch
Island Drive North
Rey, NY 10580

Robert Townsend
3000 Durand Drive
Los Angeles, CA 90068

Gary Trudeau
271 Central Park W. #10E
New York, NY 10024

Donald Trump
721 Fifth Avenue
New York, NY 10022

Ivana Trump
725 Fifth Avenue
New York, NY 10022

Ted Turner
1050 Techwood Drive
Atlanta, GA 30318

Twiggy
15 Hanover Square
4 St. George's House
London, W1R 9AJ, ENGLAND

U   U

Peter Ueberroth
184 Emerald Bay
Laguna Beach, CA 92651

Leon Uris
P.O. Box 1559
Aspen, CO 81611

V   V

Jack Valenti
1600 Eye Street N.W.
Washington, DC 20006

Abigail Van Buren
9200 Sunset Blvd. #1003
Los Angeles, CA 90069

Gloria Vanderbilt
10 Gracie Square PH
New York, NY 10018

Gore Vidal
La Rondinaia Amalfi Ravello
Salerno, ITALY

Paul A. Volcker
Prof. International Economics
Princeton University
Princeton, NJ 08544

Betsy Von Furstenberg
114 E. 28th Street #203
New York, NY 10016

Diane Von Furstenberg
745 Fifth Avenue
New York, NY 10151

Kurt Vonnegut, Jr.
228 E. 48th Street
New York, NY 10017

W   W

Mort Walker
61 Studio Court
Stamford, CT 06903

Sam Moore Walton
702 S. W. 8th Street
Bentonville, AR 72712

Lew Wasserman
911 N. Foothill Road
Beverly Hills, CA 90210

John Waters
575 - 8th Avenue #1600
New York, NY 10018

Andrew Lloyd Webber
Trump Tower
725 Fifth Avenue
New York, NY 10022

Casper W. Weinberger
60 Fifth Avenue
New York, NY 10011

Rev. Benjamin Weir
475 Riverside Drive #1201
New York, NY 10115

Dr. Ruth Westheimer
900 W. 190th Street
New York, NY 10040

Star Guide 1992-1993   Other Famous People

Thomas Wicker
c/o New York Times
229 W. 43rd Street
New York, NY 10036

Bruce Williams
c/o NBC Radio
30 Rockefeller Plaza
New York, NY 10020

Elie Wiesel
40 Boston University
745 Commonwealth Avenue
Boston, MA 02115

Bob Woodward
1150 - 15th Street N.W.
Washington, DC 20005

Herman Wouk
3255 "N" Street N.W.
Washington, DC 20007

Simon Wiesenthal
Salvtorgasse 6
1010, Vienna, 1, AUSTRIA

Steve Wozniak
21435 Summit Road
Los Gatos, CA 95030

George Will
1717 DeSales Street N.W.
Washington, DC 20036

Y   Y

Mollie Yard
1401 New York Avenue N.W.
Washington, DC 20005

Gen. Charles E. Yeager
P.O. Box 128
Cedar Ridge, CA 95924

Z   Z

Richard Zanuch
202 N. Canon Drive
Beverly Hills, CA 90210

Franco Zefferelli
9247 Swallow Drive
Los Angeles, CA 90069

Carmen Zapata
6107 Ethel Avenue
Van Nuys, CA 91405

Bob Zemeckis
1880 Century Park East #900
Los Angeles, CA 90067

Index

They're Not A Star Until
They're A Star In Star Guide™

USE THESE BOOKS
TO WRITE
FAMOUS CELEBRITIES

STAR GUIDE™ 1992–1993
Star Guide is the most reliable and up–to–date guide available for over 3200
addresses of major stars from every field: Movie and TV, Music, Sports, Politics
and other Famous People. ISBN 0-943213-04-5 and ISSN 1060-9997
ONLY $12⁹⁵ + $1⁹⁵ Postage & Handling

CELEBRITY DIRECTORY™ (1992–1993)
(4th Edition) Covers the entire spectrum of celebrities. This directory gives over
7000 celebrity addresses. If a person is famous and worth locating, it's almost
certain their address can be found in the Celebrity Directory™.
ISBN 0-943213-06-1, LC# 91-78325
ONLY $34⁹⁵ + $2⁵⁰ Postage & Handling

CELEBRITY BIRTHDAY DIRECTORY™
The authoritative directory for the birthdays of hundreds of celebrities. Use it to
send all your favorite stars a birthday greeting. ISBN 0-943213-05-3
ONLY $4⁹⁵ + $1⁹⁵ Postage & Handling

Please complete and mail to:
> **Axiom Information Resources**
> **P.O. Box 8015-T1**
> **Ann Arbor, MI 48107**
> **USA**

(Distributor inquiries welcomed)

- -

Name_____

Street_____

City _____ State _____ Zip _____

Please send _____ copy(ies) of **1992–1993 Star Guide™** at $12.95 each.

Please send _____ copy(ies) of **Celebrity Directory™ (1992-1993)** at $34.95 each.

Please send _____ copy(ies) of **Celebrity Birthday Directory™** at $4.95 ea.

Please send _____ copy(ies) ***1993–94 Star Guide™** at $12.95 each.

> *(1993–94 Edition will be available after November 1, 1992)

Payment in US currency only   Total of Order: $_____.___

                                        Postage and Handling: $_____.___
                                        Star Guide, $1.95:
Send Order To: **Celebrity Directory, $2.50:**
Axiom Information Resources   **Celebrity Birthday Directory, $1.95:**
P.O. Box 8015-T1   MI residents enclose state sales tax: $_____.___
Ann Arbor, MI 48107   (52¢ Star Guide / $1.40 Celebrity Directory/
USA   20¢ Birthday Directory)
                                        Total enclosed: $_____.___

USE THESE BOOKS
TO WRITE FAMOUS
CELEBRITIES

STAR GUIDE™ 1992–1993
Star Guide is the most reliable and up-to-date guide
available for over 3200 addresses of major stars from
every field: Movie and TV, Music, Sports, Politics and
other famous people.
ONLY $12⁹⁵ + $1⁹⁵ Postage & Handling

CELEBRITY BIRTHDAY BOOK™
The authoritative directory for the birthdays of hundreds of celebrities. Use it to send all your favorite
stars a birthday greeting.
ONLY $4⁹⁵ + $1⁹⁵ Postage & Handling

Please complete and mail to:
**Axiom Information Resources
Marketing Dept. 7T
P.O. Box 8015
Ann Arbor, MI 48107**
(Distributor inquiries welcomed)

1992-1993 STA☆ GUIDE™

OVER 3200 NAMES AND ADDRESSES
★ MOVIE STARS ★ TV STARS ★
★ VIDEO STARS ★ MUSICIANS ★
★ SPORTS CELEBRITIES ★
★ POLITICIANS ★
AND OTHER FAMOUS PEOPLE

$4⁹⁵

CELEBRITY
BIRTHDAY
DIRECTORY™

Names and Bir...
of Movie St...
T.V. Stars
and other Cele...

AIR

Name_____
Street_____
City _____ State _____ Zip _____

Please send___ copy(ies) of **1992-1993 Star Guide™**
at $12.95 each. $_____.____

Please send___copy(ies) of **Celebrity Birthday
Directory™** at $4.95 each. $_____.____
(Payment in US currency only).

Total of Order: $_____.____
Postage and Handling, $1.95: $_____.____
MI residents enclose 4% state sales tax: $_____.____
(52¢ Star Guide / 20¢ Birthday Directory)
Total enclosed: $_____.____

Please send _____ copy(ies) **1993-94 Star Guide™**
at $12.95 each.
(1993-94 Edition will be shipped in November 1992.)